STAGE
COMBAT

"THE ACTION TO THE WORD"

WILLIAM HOBBS

*with a
foreword by
Sir Laurence Olivier*

St. Martin's Press • New York

For Janet, Laurence and Edwin

Some of the material in this book is taken from
Techniques of the Stage Fight by William Hobbs,
published by Studio Vista Limited in 1967.

First published 1980
© William Hobbs 1980

For information, write: St. Martin's Press,
175 Fifth Avenue, New York, N.Y. 10010
Manufactured in the United States of America

Library of Congress Cataloging in Publication Data

Hobbs, William, 1939-
    Stage combat.

    1. Stage fighting.   2.   Stage fencing.   I.   Title
PN2071.F5H6   1981   792′.028   81-8847
ISBN 0-312-75493-0   AACR2

Set in Baskerville Old Face

Contents

Foreword

'The Master of the Fence' is a splendid title, redolent of times when *le mot juste* was *le mot le plus splendide* or to be more vaudevillian:

> 'Those days of fame,
> When a Pansy was a flower
> And a Fanny was a name.'

Mr Hobbs has gone into his task with the extremest and most loving care and, I should guess, as thoroughly as can ever have been done.

I wish he had been born before I was, so that I could have had the benefit of such an abundance of advice and knowledge of technique.

My training and exercise in the art of fence has been largely grounded on the clockwork technique of 'one, two, three; two, one, four;' or 'bish, bash, bosh; bash, bosh, bish; no, no, no, you should not be doing bosh there, it is bash first, *then* bosh, *now* then, bosh, bash, bish, then *backhand* bosh'. This sounds idiotic enough but can be quite good if you look as if you really *mean* it, and use carefully practised variations of rhythm, also with a few escapes — I mean purposely narrow escapes — some surprises here and there and a frill or two, your little fight can look quite respectable.

I have always felt very strongly that a stage fight offered the actor a unique opportunity of winning the audience, as great almost as any scene, speech or action. That Shakespeare put it high in his estimation of stage effects is proclaimed by the amount of times he trustingly leaves it to this element to provide him with his dénouements, and this, as Mr Hobbs points out, for an audience commonly practised in the art and therefore shrewdly critical of the goings on.

There is a traditional paradox in reference to stage fights 'the safer the more dangerous'. Most accidents can be attributed to hesitancies and other symptoms of not wishing to hurt your opponent.

I have in my stage fighting life been more hurt than hurting, which would seem to absolve me in principle from this weakness, though in my mind's eye I see a couple of prone spectres of the past raising themselves upon a painful elbow aghast with speechless incredulity at my effrontery in making any such assertion.

I was first caused to muse upon these matters by an incident during *Romeo and Juliet* about Christmas-time 1935. I had hurt Geoffrey Toone quite badly in the Mercutio-Tybalt bout and the poor lad had to leave the cast for some weeks on account of his thumb *hanging by a thread*. The next evening I found myself squared up to the understudy — Harry Andrews no less. Each found something about his opponent that set his nostrils aquiver, if not his foot apawing and shrill neighing assailing the air. To each was flashed that instantaneous recognition of a kindred spirit. We both knew 'they' were going to get a good fight. From then on through the run no holds were barred and sparks flew like Japanese crackers and it was more up to the audience to defend itself as best it could rather than either of us.

We were using bucklers and hand-and-a-half hilted longish swords and hardly a performance went by that the tip of one of these did not go zinging out into the auditorium to be greeted by a female shriek, an outraged masculine snort of 'look here, I say', and a sobbing exit through one of the swing doors. How the management coped with it I shall never know.

Looking back over my career now, I see it as a long, a very long chapter of almost every imaginable kind of accident, which would seem to say that either I am a bad fighter or my rule of 'the safer the more dangerous' is a load of malarkey.

Without pausing for reflection I can think of:

1 broken ankle
2 torn cartilages (1 perforce yielding to surgery)
2 broken calf muscles
3 ruptured Achilles tendons
Untold slashes including a full thrust razor-edged sword wound in the *breast* (thrilling)
Landing from considerable height, scrotum first, upon acrobat's knee
Hanging by hand to piano wire 40 feet up for some minutes (hours?) on account of unmoored rope
Hurled to the stage from 30 feet due to faultily moored rope ladder
Impalement upon jagged ply cut-outs
Broken foot bone by standing preoccupied in camera track
Broken face by horse galloping into camera while looking through finder
Near broken neck diving into net
Several shrewd throws from horses including one over beast's head into lake
One arrow shot between shinbones
Water on elbow
Water pretty well everywhere
Hands pretty well mis-shapen now through 'taking' falls
Quite a few pretended injuries while it was really gout
Near electrocution through scimitar entering studio dimmer while backing away from unwelcome interview
Etc., etc., etc.

Not to mention injuries inflicted upon my colleagues. (Memories of R. R. as Richmond, *sotto voce* but not unheard . . . 'Steady boy now', 'Easy fellow' or 'You've got two today boy . . .' 'Merely venture to submit'.)

Not to mention injuries inflicted upon my audiences.

I could go on a great deal.

Honourable scars? Well, I am not sure.

But why introduce, with a chapter of accidents and mistakes, a text book in which one is sure there are none?

Laurence Olivier

Acknowledgements

I should like to thank the following for their generous help in providing illustrations and photographs, and for giving me advice in the preparation of this book: Reg Amos, Jack Barry, John Barton, Peter Boyes A. I. Chor., Cyril Brasher, Edgar K. Bruce, Bronwen Curry F. I. Chor., the Institute of Choreology, Lesley Lindsay, the Raymond Mander and Joe Mitcheson Theatre Collection, Henry Marshall, Pollock's Toy Theatre Museum, Norman Sims, Arthur Wise and, finally, my wife Janet.

Introduction

In bygone days, when duelling was commonplace, theatre audiences must surely have been critical of stage bouts when the real thing was not an unusual occurrence. Nowadays, when the public is presented with all forms of violence, real and unreal, through the media, the job of presenting a stage fight is even more difficult. The main problem is how to give a production the effect of reality, while using only an acceptable level of violence. This level is a matter for each individual director and fight-arranger to arrive at, according to a particular interpretation of a play, and as responsible members of society. It is not part of the aim of this book to enter into a debate on violence in the media, nor indeed does it set out to deal with the special additional techniques and considerations needed to present fights for films and television. Much of what follows, however, in the way of analysis and preparation, as well as of technique, is equally applicable to stage, film or television. For example, the teaching of moves needs to be done with the same diligence whatever the form of presentation, but it is the selection of what is done which will often differ. The careful selection of details that can be specially focused on by means of a close camera shot, and the use of special effects, are obvious examples of the additional possibilities available to the fight director when filming. Also, in films and television, in contrast to the stage, special stunt-work is possible, as is the use of stunt doubles for actors, where it is necessary to assist the end result.

The shooting of a television or film fight scene — after, of course, a proper rehearsal period — is often a one-day operation, which permits an actor to put his 'all' into the scene, in

the knowledge that he can then forget it completely and go for a drink! On the stage, fights have to be performed effectively and safely night after night, which means the actor cannot afford to become sloppy, or to take chances. Naturally, fights in any of the media have to be performed with safety, so in fact a code of conduct — or rather, a disciplined attitude and method of working — is equally applicable to television, the stage or films. However, the main concern of this book is to offer overall guidelines to help in the work of tackling the presentation of a *stage* fight.

The challenge of presenting a convincing, exciting and imaginative fight may on the face of it be a daunting prospect to the inexperienced, not unlike the fitting together of a jigsaw puzzle. There are many moves and tricks available to the actors and the fight director (arranger). Thus, it is only when the various components, such as the creation and selection of moves which relate to character, the sharpening of the actors' skill and the proper forwarding of the story, are all put imaginatively together that the fight scene can be considered to work. Then there are tricks of the trade, such as the simulation of the sound of a punch, the secretion and showing of blood at the right moment, the masking from the audience of the moment of a blow's supposed connection and the substitution of safe replica weapons in place of the real ones for a potentially dangerous move — all have their place in creating a few moments, or minutes, of theatrical illusion — or magic.

It is not my intention to formulate a rigid set of rules, for when it comes to arranging fights each new play or production makes new demands that will involve new answers. The only rules which are always applicable are those combining safety and the illusion of reality. The few fundamental moves which are explained later in the book are included not so much to teach as to serve as illustrations of the care, precision and technique which have to be achieved, no matter how simple a sequence. To learn physical skills from a book, without additional training under a qualified tutor, is not, I believe, practicable. It is therefore my intention that what follows will act as a guide to the inexperienced, so that they may put their own ideas into operation more smoothly. I also hope the manual will help in promoting a professional attitude and way of thinking about the task of performing and arranging fights that will be useful in demonstrating the range of exciting possibilities and challenges which are open to directors, actors and fight-arrangers alike.

1. Background

The further back one goes into history, the less is known about actual methods of fighting and how these were transferred into theatrical requirements. The interest and attention accorded to stage fights is by no means new. It is recorded in the *Playgoer* of 1903 that Esmé Berringer 'had the honour of taking the chair at Captain Hutton's interesting lecture at the Playgoers Club on Stage Fights'. Until quite recently it was the custom in theatres and drama schools for 'A Master of Fence' to be employed to teach and stage fights. His knowledge and experience of the theatre and actors was in most cases limited, to say the least. Alternatively, an actor who was able to fence would be told 'you can do the fight bit', with not even a credit appearing in the programme! If a fencing master was employed it was the director of the play who more often than not would put the fight into dramatic form, the fencing master being only required to set the strokes and rehearse the moves. Today, with experts at everything popping up in all branches of theatre, fight-arranging too has become a specialist activity, and stage-fight directors need theatrical experience which they can effectively combine with some kind of martial-art expertise.

In Victorian times, when the play demanded that the duel should be played, a number of well-known routines were often used, the most appropriate being selected according to the requirements of a play, but not specially created as nowadays. These were referred to by the profession of that time as 'The Square Eights', 'The Round Eights', 'The Glasgow Tens' (known in England as 'The Long Elevens'), and even one called 'The Drunk Combat'. All these routines were made up from a series of cuts — not cuts as we know them today, but rather whacks at the opponent's blade. These could be repeated as often as required all over the stage — rather in the fashion that children play at sword-fighting with sticks; the older actor will undoubtedly recall these practices which were popular at one time.

The great Master of Fence of the mid-Victorian period was Felix Bertrand, who set many stage combats, including the duel between Tree and Fred Terry in *Hamlet*, Forbes Robertson's *Macbeth* and *Hamlet*, Ben Greet's *Nelson's Enchantress*, and Wyndom's *Cyrano de Bergerac*; in fact, many of the leading actors of the day were pupils of Bertrand. Besides Tree, Forbes Robertson, Fred Terry and Ben Greet, these included Irving, Bancroft and Lewis Waller, as well as such writers as Thackeray and Dickens. Actors of the day considered the ability to fence an important asset, which must of course have made Bertrand's task much easier when it came to setting a fight. It is worth recording in this context that in the duel between Irving and Squire Bancroft in the play *The Dead Heart*, only the final hit was actually planned, so it seems fairly obvious that both men must have been experts with the blade, and as such would have been able to fence without trying for an actual hit — until the prepared and well-rehearsed final thrust. By today's standards, this may seem hardly a professional way of going about things, but this fight set all of London talking, and no wonder! It is even more remarkable when one learns that Irving was quite short-sighted — so short-sighted, in fact, that it is said that when he was playing a scene with an actress who was portraying a blind girl he accidentally dropped his glasses on the stage, and the 'blind' girl was the only one of the two who could 'see' to retrieve them! With such an affliction, it is almost incredible, and certainly to his credit (or luck), that he was able to perform such fights on the stage night after night, without any serious mishap.

Flying sparks were at this time considered an important feature of a fight. Irving was much enamoured of such effects, and would attach flints to the blade of his sword in order to achieve them. However, with the advent of electricity, in his pursuit of even greater 'fireworks', he actually had the weapons wired up to make sure they would constantly throw off sparks. Although it is not known whether any of his company was actually electrocuted, it wasn't long before he was using rubber insulation on the handles of the swords!

In the nineteenth and early twentieth century combats were a thriving and much-loved part of the theatrical scene, and many a bad play was devised as an excuse for 'a terrific combat'. Even the women got in on the act — Miss Esmé Berringer called upon to fight in *At the Point of the Sword* was one example. Charles Dickens, himself a pupil of Bertrand, watched rehearsals of the combat in *Hamlet* between Fechter and Herman Vezin, and was sufficiently fascinated by stage fighting to include in *Nicholas Nickleby* a fight routine which was to be presented by the Crummles' Company. The fight must surely have been typical of the kind of combat relished by the audience who patronized productions by the many actor-managers of the day:

'Nicholas was prepared for something odd, but not for something quite so odd as the sight he encountered. At the upper end of the room, were a couple of boys, one of them very tall and the other very short, both dressed as sailors — or at least as theatrical sailors, with belts, buckles, pigtails, and pistols complete — fighting what is called in playbills a terrific combat, with two of those short broad-swords with basket hilts which are commonly used at our minor theatres. The short boy had gained a great advantage over the tall boy, who was reduced to mortal strait, and both were overlooked by a large heavy man, perched against a corner of a table, who emphatically adjured them to strike a little more fire out of the swords, and they couldn't fail to bring the house down, on the very first night . . .

'. . . The two combatants went to work afresh, and chopped away until the swords emitted a shower of sparks: to the great satisfaction of Mr Crummles, who appeared to consider this a very great point indeed. The engagement commenced with about two hundred chops administered by the short sailor and the tall sailor alternately, without producing any particular result, until the short sailor was chopped down on one knee; but this was nothing to him, for he worked himself about on the one knee with the assistance of his left hand, and fought most desperately until the tall sailor chopped his sword out of his grasp. Now, the inference was, that the short sailor, reduced to this extremity, would give in at once and cry quarter, but, instead of that, he all of a sudden drew a large pistol from his belt and presented it at the face of the tall sailor, who was so overcome at this (not expecting it) that he let the short sailor pick up his sword and begin again. Then, the chopping recommenced, and a variety of fancy chops were administered on both sides; such as chops dealt with the left hand, and under the leg, and over the right shoulder, and over the left; and when the short sailor made a vigorous cut at the tall sailor's legs, which would have shaved them clean off if it had taken effect, the tall sailor jumped over the short sailor's sword, wherefore to balance the matter, and make it all fair, the tall sailor administered the same cut, and the short sailor jumped over *his* sword. After this, there was a good deal of dodging about, the hitching up of the inexpressibles in the absence of braces, and then the short sailor (who was the moral character evidently, for he always had the best of it) made a violent demonstration and closed in with the tall sailor, who, after a few unavailing struggles, went down, and expired in great torture as the short sailor put his foot upon his breast, and bored a hole in him through and through.

' "That'll be a double *encore* if you take care, boys," said Mr **Crummles**. "You had better get your wind now and change your clothes . . ."

' "What do you think of that, sir?" inquired Mr Crummles.

' "Very good, indeed — capital," answered Nicholas.

' "You won't see such boys as those very often, I think," said Mr Crummles.

'Nicholas assented — observing, that if they were a little better match —

' "Match!" cried Mr Crummles.

' "I mean if they were a little more of a size," said Nicholas, explaining himself.

' "Size!" repeated Mr Crummles; "why it's the essence of the combat that there should be a foot or two between them. How are you to get up the sympathies of the audience in a legitimate manner, if there isn't a little man contending against a big one — unless there's at least five to one, and we haven't hands enough for that business in our company . . ."

' "It's the main point," said Mr Crummles.'

There are three points from the above extract of particular interest. One is the mention of the type of swords used, 'short broad-swords with basket hilts which are commonly used at our minor theatres'. This could be taken as a 'dig' at the minor theatres for always using the same weapons no matter what the period of the play. Secondly, it is noteworthy to read of the use of surprise when the tall sailor disarms the shorter one, who there-upon thrusts a pistol in the face of the tall sailor, and is able to retrieve his sword and get on with it again. Something of a cliché these days, no doubt, but it was obviously what the audience of the time loved. Thirdly, it seems that the best 'fancy chops' were saved to nearly the end (building up the audience's fervour!), prior to the short sailor making a particularly violent demonstration for the dénouement. Crummles knew his stuff!

It was often the practice for fight moves and strokes to be handed down — a set sequence already known by the actors saved a great deal of time and rehearsal. This was hardly creative theatre, but at least it could be performed (which is probably the reason for its being done) with the maximum confidence and fury, sparks flying in all directions. The audience demanded an exciting combat, and must have shown their displeasure in no uncertain manner if they witnessed anything at all tentative through under-rehearsal. The type of actor-manager who would instruct his company to deliver their lines no nearer than arm's length from him must also have expected his opponent in the combat to be able to perform a well-known routine with competence at the first rehearsal.

2. Analysis and Construction

Quite obviously, it is essential before beginning work on any fight arrangement — no matter how slight the skirmish — to know the play and to understand the function of the characters. No two people move or react in the same way, and the personality of each of the characters will determine the way they fight, and govern everything they do during the fight sequence. People who behave in a distinctly individual way throughout a play cannot and must not merge in personality when fighting. Broadly speaking, if careful consideration is given to a man's physique, intellect and personality, an idea will be formed of the probable way he will move and fight.

Clearly, to have two or three minutes of unceasing sword-whacking will be pretty meaningless. All it conveys to an audience is 'this is where these two men fight', and that is all. It will add little to the development of the play. Even in a well-known play, where the outcome of the fight is common knowledge, the audience should entertain an occasional doubt as to whether or not the author's known intentions are going to be fulfilled.

Initial discussions with the director, set and costume designer are essential before planning anything. Particular note should be paid to costume and set designs for they can both aid and hamper the action. It may be possible to influence the designs at an early stage, but once the making is underway, usually the combat will have to be moulded to fit in with them, and not the other way round. Set and costume alterations can be expensive — fight moves are not!

Having decided upon an approach to the fight, which arises out of a firm grasp of the play and its characters, the next task is to devise a rough shape. Occasionally an author will give a shape to you. This is of enormous help, for the moments of action, as in *Hamlet*, are interspersed with dialogue and business. The dramatist tells the story for you — or rather he indicates very firmly how he wants 'his' fight to be — so the dramatic shape is already defined. The peaks are there, and it is the task of the arranger to work out how he leads up to them.

The majority of authors, however, give little or no help in this way, so then a shape has to be created. By this I mean dividing a fight up into phases of action, pauses and incidents, depending on how it is felt it should run. People do not inevitably try to knock the hell out of each other non-stop when their lives are at stake. In a certain type of situation, when one mistake may mean death, they may be cautious, and therefore there will be pauses. The excitement of a dead stop after a piece of really fast action, with neither character daring to move a muscle, can be tremendous, like two rattlesnakes poised for an attack.

So there is action and pause, action and pause. This in itself is a crude shape, and the length of each of these phases will vary. There might be a long piece of action, followed by a short pause, and then a single movement or stroke followed by a longer pause, not just for its own sake, but where such a pause or piece of action has grown out of the situation. It is impossible to make rules, for all depends on the text and the story to be told. Some fights are over in a flash — they are not really fights at all, just killings, without much analysis or construction. A quick stab or two, gurgle and *finito*. Mostly, though, there will be variations, brought about either by outside influence (other people on stage, scenery, props, etc.) or by the main characters themselves. Incidents will disrupt the pattern of organized sword-play. Whatever the emotions, they involve changes, which provide variety, and variety and invention are the essential ingredients of all combats.

Finally, although the director will usually give the arranger a free hand in conducting the fight episode, the combat will nevertheless have to be in accordance with the agreed concept, so it is important to attend rehearsals of the complete play to enable the fight to grow truly out of the whole, and not to be a mini-spectacle divorced from the rest of the piece.

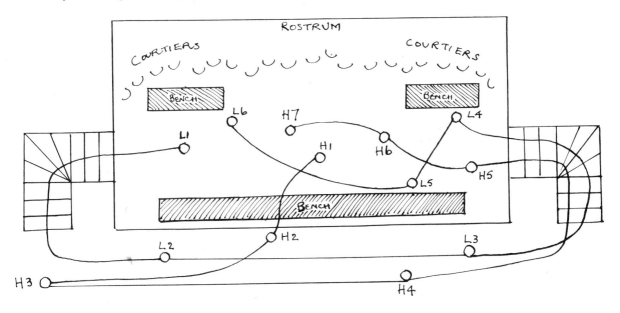

3. Movement and Patterns

I have always been very conscious of the pictures being presented to an audience throughout the fight. Here I have in mind two distinctly separate things: the actual patterns made by weapons and bodies, and the overall movements of people about the stage.

Dealing, perversely, with the second subject first, it should be obvious that except when two sloggers are hammering away at each other, fighters hard at it will not remain in fixed position. They will move because they have to, either 'controlled' or 'out of control', for numerous different reasons. In attack, or in retreat, they will move, fast or slowly depending upon what is happening; they may move to gain the advantage of height, to induce their opponent to make some error in order to counter-attack, or simply in panic. So too on stage, always dependent on the situation, the characters will move in various ways, and these moves will be planned, (according to the ideas of the arranger, actors and director) to grow from an analysis of the text and characters. The object is to let the overall movements evolve without imposing them too rigidly, while at the same time creating a variety of positioning. The good arranger will have a feeling for the emotions of the characters which will lead him to block moves in accordance with the actors' ideas and conception. Allowing all this, there are then certain technical requirements. It is important to plot moves in such a way (a) as to position them in order to exert their greatest effect on the audience, ensuring that the best are not hidden or viewed from the wrong angle, while at the same time masking any tricks which should not be seen; and (b) to make the most of a variety of positioning, changing this wherever possible in the light of the situation in order to present a change of picture and to maintain the audience's interest.

The reader will notice that in this (the last violent part of the fight), as great a use of the stage as possible has been made, and a pattern of movement has been created. The on-stage spectators' moves are too involved to relate here, but their diverse movements, in, around, between and away from the two protagonists were used to accentuate the sudden danger of the situation, thus creating visually and emotionally a more powerful climax.

As to the movement of bodies and various strokes of the weapons, they are making patterns all the time. When working on the initial construction, it is worthwhile spending time on ensuring choreographic variety to create pleasing patterns, which consist of logical movements. The audience will lose interest when there is constant repetition of the same moves — unless, of course, the situation is such that a repetitive bludgeoning effect is called for.

4. Fight Orchestration

To discuss a fight in musical terms, and to talk about its rhythms, will probably sound incongruous, and perhaps pretentious. However, possibly because of a vaguely musical background (I own up to having been a leading chorister in a cathedral choir school, more handy at fighting off unwelcome missiles during the sermon than rendering a devotional *Fight the Good Fight*), I have always been conscious that most well-constructed fights have changes of rhythm and are 'orchestrated' in a way not unlike a musical score. For example, a fight may, like a piece of music, start in low key at a slow tempo and gradually gain in momentum and pitch, arriving eventually at the equivalent of a clash of cymbals. This can be followed, perhaps, by a period of uneasy calm shattered occasionally by phrases of 'staccato'; then *rallentando* until the next crescendo, and so on until the final climax. Without this orchestration, or shape, a fight will not only run the risk of being excessively dull, but will probably emerge as an unorganized mess.

How often has one seen a stage fight which contains virtually the same rhythm and feeling throughout the entire sequence, and lacks any change or variety of mood! To extend the musical analogy further, it is as though the actors are performing a fight equivalent to *Chopsticks* over and over again with relentless monotony. The restriction of every combat to the same kind of tempo, without variety or punctuation, will have a soporific effect, and will ultimately — albeit unconsciously — lose the audience's interest. There is no dogma to define the positioning for changes of mood and rhythm; all that is necessary is an awareness of the need for such

variations from time to time, as the situation requires. In my experience, it is only when one is in actual rehearsal that rhythmic changes of feeling are easily effected, and the need for such changes perceived. They can be planned in advance, but this is limiting to creative ideas and the organic growth of the episode.

I am of course talking generally when I say that various extraneous sounds and noises are an additional necessity to the fight, as well as changes of mood and atmosphere, and are as vital as are percussive moments and tonal variation to a symphony or concerto. Obviously the majority of stage skirmishes cannot be enacted truthfully and effectively if the only sound to be heard is the faint clash of weapons wielded by silent combatants. Murmurs and shouts from the onlookers as they react to what is going on, screams, bells — in fact, any noises that derive solely from the fight alone — will not detract from the action, but will support and heighten it. The fighters too will usually need to share in this 'percussion', for without sound of some kind the effect can be like a silent film of the Keystone Kops — all dash and go, with no piano in the pit. In films the sound of steel on steel often has to be dubbed on after shooting, to heighten the effect and to create excitement. Occasionally when I have asked an actor for a shout at a particular moment he has questioned the validity of such a direction, not feeling the need for such an expression. If, however, he had seen the film *The Seven Samurai*, or fenced to four-all, when everything depends on the final hit, he would understand how a shout comes readily and naturally to a combatant launching an attack after a period of tension. When energy is held back, and out of desperation is

suddenly released, the shout is a natural extension of the attacking move. Until the actor is able to execute the moves of a fight confidently so that they become second nature, and the acting performance of the fight takes over, he may find that such a shout or shouts may feel alien. This is natural, but it is important at some stage of rehearsal that the sequence be acted through vocally as well as physically, because the vocal aspect can be too easily forgotten, and its significance lost. I am of course referring to most fight situations. There are naturally exceptions which require different handling.

To sum up, and to clarify this rather difficult analogy, one need only to listen to a tiny snatch of a well-known musical piece to get the idea. H. C. Colles says, 'It was a favourite device of Beethoven suddenly, when one expected familiar things, to open up a new vista of harmony and shake off the fetters of convention. Since the coda is the place where one begins to foresee the end, he particularly loves to give something unforeseen there.' Colles goes on to talk about the way Beethoven uses an element of surprise in the finale of the Sonata in C Minor (op. 10 No. 1), where just before the end he checks the flow to introduce the second subject which gets slower and slower in the remote key of D flat major. He gradually lulls his hearers to rest, and then, with a sweeping arpeggio, picks up the thread of his discourse and makes a rapid end — so rich and varied are the sudden transitions of Beethoven's codas that one might fill a volume in examining them.

So too with fights — dark and light passages, punctuation — in fact, contrasts, change and variety.

5. The Element of Surprise

An alternative chapter heading would be 'The Quest for the Unobvious', for in dealing with combats, inevitably much the same situation is often repeated under various guises in different plays. To find the right approach for this or that particular scene may require a real search for an idea which will bring the fight in question uniquely to life. Take for example the commonplace hero/villain situation — D'Artagnan v. Rochefort, Robin Hood v. Guy of Gisbourne or even Macbeth v. Macduff, all climactic fights coming at the end of the story. Different weapons will probably be used, according to the historical period in which each play is set, which helps — as does the involvement of very different characters — to produce varied treatment. Nonetheless, the danger remains of a single approach to certain fights, owing to the basic similarity of the situations. With the richness of background of a play like *Macbeth* there really is no excuse for the fight not to grow truly out of the story, but consider the case where the author

has given little character information upon which to build the fight. Then you have a cardboard situation, and the only way this can be brought to life is by searching for ideas and possibilities which can lift the scene into reality and even surprise an audience, by the use of the unexpected. Life will be brought to the fight by ideas — movements alone, however well performed, are really insufficient. To repeat well-tried moves and even ideas in different plays with a fundamentally similar situation is the easy way out, particularly when a piece may only demand a light-hearted skirmish. This can never be the creative art of fight-direction. The concern is with characterization and to deal with a scene properly according to the story. Blocking out the right moves is important, of course, but only a part of the job. The discovery and presentation of little personality quirks and eccentricities, the moments of unexpected invention, the element of surprise, the enaction of the unusual, not just for its own sake but because such a thing *could* happen, even

though it be not explicit in the text — all these give the real texture to a fight scene. The incorporation of the unobvious, even though this must always be dependent upon the truth of the scene, will enrich the fight and give it life, particularly in those cases where the author has given a stock situation without a great deal of information for the fight director to go on. Like any choreographer, the director of a combat scene will have a repertoire of moves which he will employ, dependent on the situation. These moves he will employ in different permutations, and perhaps with flair and variety, but still in the end it is not these, but the IDEAS behind them which are limitless. It is perfectly feasible, even within a set structure, to shed new light on familiar situations, while remaining faithful to the text. It is these ideas incorporated within a fight structure, just as much as the skill and exciting performance of the par-ticipants, that will enhance the combat and give it dramatic shape. The two requirements go hand in hand. The fast attacks of the fighters and the ring of steel are all very well, but can be boring unless supported by originally thought-out happenings that could only be displayed by particular combatants in a particular situation. Of course, it is not only ideas involving the fighters them-selves which matter. The discretionary use of other characters on stage, lighting effects, props, sound effects and music can all enhance, clarify and invigorate a situation when used imaginatively.

So then, to sum up, changing focus by the use of ideas which are in keeping with the text, inventing through the characters, the situation and the times in which the play is set are very important facets of an approach by which one can bring a fight scene to life, and give it mean-ing and dramatic structure.

6. Safety Precautions and Method of Rehearsing

Having planned the fight in rough and given it overall shape, it is imperative to employ throughout rehearsals certain safety procedures. Here the vital consideration is to ensure that the fight is not accident-prone, for the safety of the players must of course come before all else. No matter how appealing certain business or movements may be, if they present any possible risk they must be revised or if necessary rejected, for it is essential that the actors feel confident in the moves they are given, and in their ability to carry them out. It is paradoxical that a fundamentally safe move can be performed dangerously, and a dangerous move executed safely.

Provided that a well-rehearsed drill and precision routine are faithfully maintained, safety can be achieved, even at full speed. Moves and positions must be carefully worked out and rehearsed, for discipline and control are the very basis upon which a safe fight depends. Rehearsal time is another all-important factor contributing to the safety and success of any stage fight. It is impossible to create anything worthwhile with insufficient rehearsal, and attempts to do so are likely either to prove dangerous, or to look amateurish, or both. Very few actors are trained in a martial art, and therefore there may sometimes be a certain reluctance or even fear in the case of a nervous actor, when called upon to participate in a fight. With this in mind, it is essential that confidence is built up gradually, and nothing rushed.

The first stage of rehearsing a sword-fight should be concerned with the synchronization of footwork with the various movements of attack and defence. For example, when one person takes a movement forward the other must take a corresponding move backward, and vice versa, so that at all times (except when purposely out of distance or in close), the same amount of space between the two is maintained. It should then follow that provided the actors start at a safe distance, it will be preserved throughout an exchange. Accidents can occur for many reasons, including getting too close, and when this happens movements are inclined to get muddled and blades to miss, thereby forcing the actors into unrehearsed and inaccurate movements. One fundamental safety precaution I have always employed, although it may not be apparent to an audience, is for the actors to work out of distance. That is to say, when one makes an attack the opponent's body is out of reach, but the blades are just able to make contact. This not only means that the point of a blade is short of the target but it forces the attacker to stretch right over in order to make blade-contact, thereby creating far more dynamic movements.

Another basic safety measure to employ in the planning of strokes is to avoid any movement which goes across the face. An unlucky blow taken on the hand may be painful, but a similarly misguided blow in the region of the face or head could be much more serious.

From the very beginning it will be possible to work to a definite, well-defined rhythm. The establishment of such a rhythm is of tremendous importance, for no matter how fast the fight eventually becomes, it will always be firmly supported by an

19

inbuilt feeling of timing. Actors in a fight are like acrobats performing a feat; timing and rhythm are essential. Each actor's movements cannot be thought of as individual, but must merge together to resemble an incredibly well-oiled machine, where the different cogs work together in unison.

Most actors prefer to have the entire fight set as quickly as possible, so that they know the work that lies ahead of them. Having done this, it is a good idea to start rehearsing a phase at a time, working on a new phase as the actors grow confident with the last. The fight should be rehearsed every day until such time as it can be done right through without stopping. At this point originally set positions and movements should be checked — though, of course, a constant watch should be kept throughout. The fight should not be speeded up too soon, or left too late; usually actors will speed up of their own accord as the moves become familiar. It is, however, potentially disastrous to speed up before a movement is seen to be repeatedly executed in a safe fashion. What then is a safe fashion?

Attacks should be made lightly, and the actors should learn to pull a stroke, so that if by accident an attack is not parried they are able to hold it back. In a cutting stroke the effort should be channelled forward in such a way that the blade as it were ricochets past the opponent once it has met his blade. The real effort then goes past the adversary and is not directed at him, but to an audience the effect is just the same. Strokes, indeed, must never be made in a heavy-handed manner. With sword-play the wearing of fencing masks during rehearsals is of course optional, but I believe their use inclines to foster a false sense of security. Better by far to rely on discipline, control and technique,

which, unlike masks, will afford a real security, remaining through all performances.

There is a school of thought which believes that it is safer to aim a stroke slightly away from the part of the body one is intending to hit. I strongly disagree with this idea, for I have found that it is far safer for the defender to know *exactly* where the attack is coming. Otherwise the attacker is going to spend all his concentration on making strokes which just miss the target, leaving the defender to guess where these misses will come, and making parries which are likely to miss, resulting in the actors being thrown, and possibly causing accidents. I would stress that my main concern in teaching actors really to aim for the body is to *avoid* accidents, even though it is only when strokes are correctly aimed that intention — and therefore reality — is achieved.

Lastly, it should not be overlooked that certain types of actors can be a danger both to themselves and to others — one such is the type who will throw himself into a fight more than is necessary, and probably in an uncontrolled and therefore potentially dangerous manner. The other, and equally dangerous man is the actor who through lack of confidence makes tentative moves. The positive and certain performer is always best, provided at the same time he acts with intention, discipline and control.

Points to remember with regard to safety procedure:

1. Never attempt to speed up too soon. For the sake of safety and the building up of actors' confidence, take all the time possible at a moderate rhythm. Speeding up a fight should be a gradual process.

2. Always work in good light.

3. At all times wear shoes that won't slip or slide, and if you are in

costume ensure that shoes have rubber soles.

4. In sword-play concentrate on never getting too close through undisciplined footwork.

5. Check that all weapon handles are covered with some non-slip material, preferably leather. A sword hilt of bare metal held in a hot, sticky hand is likely to slip and go out of control. Resin for the hands and feet is an added safeguard.

6. Check that the floor is not slippery.

7. If possible for sword work wear gloves — preferably made of soft chamois leather.

8. Sweep the stage before performance, and give particular attention to removing debris — tacks and screws, etc. — which could prove hazardous.

9. Limber up and rehearse the fight before every performance. This should be done with the actual weapons, as per performance, and not merely marked through casually.

10. Never change to different swords or weapons without proper rehearsal, for the difference in weight or balance can be a potential danger.

A Warning Note

Extract from *The Sketch*, 19 August 1896. Re: The Tragedy at the Novelty Theatre:

'Both ancient and modern records can show many a stage mishap, though not often of so serious a character as that which has just occurred. Upon the night of the first production of H. J. Byron's powerful drama *Michael Strogoff* at the Adelphi, 15 March 1881, Mr Charles Warner, in the title role, bearing dispatches to the Russian Grand Duke, was set upon by Ivan Ogareff, the villain of the piece, played by Mr James Fernandez, and a duel with daggers ensued, in the excitement of which Mr Warner was badly wounded in the hand. But, with admirable pluck, he kept the injured hand behind him, and, though sick and faint from the pain and loss of blood, struggled on till the curtain fell. Only the other day, too, Mr Gordon Craig, playing Macduff, "laid on" with such an excess of zeal that the unfortunate Macbeth suffered somewhat severely about the hand; but not so badly as the unlucky Macduff who lost a couple of fingers in his stage fight with the Macbeth of the great Macready.

'Barry Sullivan once attacked Richard the Third with such vigour that his opponent's sword was dashed from his hand, and they were within an ace of a bad accident; and Mr William Terriss has had at least one unpleasant experience of stage duels. Even more remarkable, in its way, was an incident which occurred in Stockholm early in the sixteenth century. The actor who played the part of Longinus in *The Mystery of the Passion*, and had to pierce Christ on the Cross, was so transported with the spirit of the action that he actually killed the other actor. The King, who was present, was so angry that he leaped on the stage and cut off the head of Longinus; and, finally the people, who had been pleased with the actor's zeal, were so infuriated with the King that they turned upon him and slew him — a veritable tragedy of tragedies.

'In an amateur performance of *Romeo and Juliet*, at the Cathedral Schools, Manchester on 31 March 1891, Tybalt, making a lunge past Romeo, unhappily passed his sword through the body of the youth, with, of course, fatal results.

'Many years ago an Italian artist named Dombardi, who was playing in *Antigone*, had to turn his sword from his father's breast to his own, and in the excitement of the moment plunged it into his body with fatal results. Once in a Chinese Theatre two actors fought a stage duel in earnest from love of the same woman, one being killed before the audience; but cases such as this of deliberate murder are rare. Only a few years ago Mr Barton McGuckin, singing in *Rienzi* at Liverpool, had a narrow escape, one of the crowd approaching him with upraised daggers losing his footing, and falling forward, the dagger passing through Mr McGuckin's arm, and slightly penetrating his breast.'

7. Sword Strokes, Some Basic Movements and Their Execution

The reader who has at any time fenced will recognize many of the following movements as similar to those used in the modern sport. However, in almost every instance there are major differences to make them more suitable for the stage from the point of view of effectiveness and safety. It is not possible to cover every stroke and movement within the scope of this book; what follows is intended merely as a basis, and the movements have been chosen with the beginner in mind. While one should remember that every period in history has a different technique according to the weapons used, a straightforward fight could nonetheless be developed using the moves described, and it will depend upon the imagination of the planner as to the effectiveness of the end result.

Stance (Fig 1)
This, like everything else, depends on character and situation, and each period of history has a different stance. In general, however, a good balanced position is with the feet fairly far apart and with knees slightly bent. This enables movements forward and backward to be executed with speed, while still maintaining balance. The feet do not need to be in a fencer's strict right-angled position, for we are not concerned with modern fencing, but to be well balanced and nimble-footed is important. It will be found that the most comfortable position for the body in most sword-fighting situations is about three-quarters on to one's opponent.

Fig 1

The Lunge *(Fig 2)*

The lunge is used in attack to reach your opponent. It is executed by pushing off from the back leg and flexing it from its bent position to a straight one. At the same time the front foot is kicked forward, so that it moves from its original position about two feet (for a man of average height). As in modern fencing, as an aid to balance the left hand should at the same time be dropped down and straightened, with the palm turned up until it is in line with the back leg. In a full lunge position the front knee will be over the front heel and there will be a straight line from the front knee to the back foot.

Fig 2

The Grip *(Figs 3 and 4)*

Unless the sword is very heavy, a general all-purpose grip is with the thumb lying straight on top of the handle and with the index finger underneath. The handle rests in the second phalanx of the forefinger, and the other three fingers hold the handle in place resting on the side. This position facilitates control, and it is better for the fingers not to be curled around the hilt.

When a heavier weapon is used it may be found necessary for the handle to be fully gripped, by wrapping the hand completely around it.

Fig 3

Fig 4

The Basic System of Attack and Parry

To set down the various methods of attack and defence through the ages would require a book on its own. Assuming that the arranger will do the necessary research into a particular period, the actor's task is to familiarize himself with the deployment of the weapons. Generally speaking, techniques of modern fencing (with some notable exceptions, such as the lunge and as an aid to eighteenth-century smallsword play) are not particularly useful for the purpose of stage combat. Fencing moves are for the most part unsafe, due to the fact that the modern fencer is trained actually to score *hits*, while the stage fighter has only to *appear* to be out to kill. Also, modern fencing looks on the stage exactly what it is, and is therefore useless in a historical piece. The number of fencing scenes in contemporary plays is to say the least small. So, having put forward what cannot be used, what is the range of options open to the arranger?

Fundamentally, I employ a very simple system of parry and attack, which is adaptable to most periods, and is easy to teach even to absolute novices. The methods are as safe as is humanly possible, provided that the principles laid down are strictly observed. Other moves are added to the basic strokes to give greater pictorial variety and elaboration. The safety procedures are these:

1. As mentioned in the previous chapter, to work (except when otherwise planned) out of distance, so that the attacker in a full lunge cannot reach the body of the defender, but is still near enough to make blade-contact.

2. All cutting strokes are pulled so that no strength is directed at the receiver.

3. As also mentioned previously, no movement ever crosses the face, whether in attack or in defence, even when the combatants are out of distance.

4. A horizontal parry meets a vertical attack, and a horizontal attack meets a vertical parry, which

ensures that both parties know exactly the angle at which a stroke is coming, and that the attacking blade does not ricochet off the parry.

Parry Positions

For convenience sake, and for use with the symbols given on p. 79, I have given the following parry positions numbers to avoid confusion with their modern fencing counterparts, as they are for the most part not quite the same. There are a number of alternative positions which vary according to the period, but the following are most commonly employed.

The head parry and the two shoulder parries differ from the equivalent fencing positions in that they are pushed further forward, and away from the body, to make for the utmost safety. The two flank parries, which are pure modern fencing positions, will differ too if heavy weapons are employed, as it will be necessary to push these forward and away from the body also, in order to meet the weightier attack that may come with a heavier weapon. If the parry is too near the body the force of a slightly heavier attack which is insufficiently pulled could go through the parry. Of course, when the participants are properly trained this will not apply, as attack will not be made in a heavy-handed fashion. Parries look far more theatrically effective if they are not passive positions, but really moving into the set position to ward off an oncoming attack. It will be found on certain occasions that if one leans away from the attack when defending the result will be more telling.

The method of making any parry is to meet the top half of the opposing blade nearest the point, with the bottom half of the defending blade nearest to the guard. Here one has fullest command of the opponent's blade, as since it is near the

hand, one has more strength, and therefore control of the weapon.

With all parries use the outside edge of the blade to meet the attack, and never the flat. Edge should meet edge.

Parry 1 — the Head Parry *(Figs 5 & 6)*

This parry is made with the blade of the sword absolutely parallel to the ground. The sword is pushed as high as possible away from the head, and at the same time forward from the face. The hand will be held to the front, with the finger-nails towards the opponent. The action of lifting the sword to meet the attack should be smooth, and the muscles of the arm and shoulder should be relaxed, for to tense up will slow down the following movement. This applies to all parries.

Fig 5   Fig 6

Parry 1a — Head Parry *(Figs 7 & 8)*

This is an alternative parry to the last, and as a variation is often useful. However, for reasons of safety the novice would be well advised not to use this parry if the previous one could be employed equally well. To make the parry, lift the sword arm as before, but on this occasion turn the back of the hand to the opponent, while making the part of the blade nearest the hilt cover the head. The hand will be to the left of the face, and forward from it.

Fig 7   Fig 8

Parry 2 — Right Shoulder Parry *(Figs 9 & 10)*

The blade in this instance is vertical to the floor, and is again pushed forward so that the strong part of the blade is covering the part to be protected. The hand is held just below shoulder-height, with the knuckles three-quarters on to the opponent.

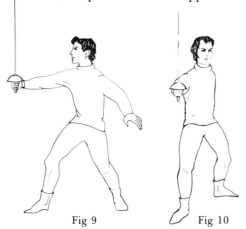

Fig 9   Fig 10

Parry 3 — Left Shoulder Parry *(Figs 11 & 12)*

Exactly the same as for parry 2, only on the left side this time, with the back of the hand three-quarters to the opponent and the palm facing oneself.

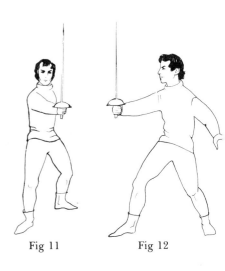

Fig 11   Fig 12

Parry 4 — Right Flank Parry *(Figs 13 & 14)*

The hand is held waist-high, just a little lower than the elbow, and the palm is turned down towards the floor. The blade is in a diagonal line, so that the strong part of the blade is covering the flank area, and the elbow is about a hand's breadth away from the body.

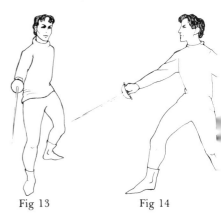

Fig 13   Fig 14

Parry 5 — Left Flank Parry *(Figs 15 & 16)*

The palm of the hand is now turned up, and the hand has moved across to the left of the body, again about waist-high. The sword-blade is in a similar diagonal, and the elbow a hand's breadth from the body.

Circular Parries

Circular parries mainly used with point weapons can add pictorial variety, but unless the performer is experienced they should only be made from parry positions 4 and 5, for from positions 2 and 3 they could be dangerous, as the opposing point can be swept into the face. Generally they should be used with a light sword, although they are sometimes permissible with a heavier weapon — but then the movement needs to be enlarged.

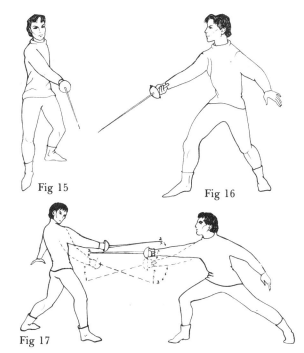

Fig 15

Fig 16

Circular Parry from position 4
(Fig 17)

Imagine that one has two duellists, and that B has made a cut to A's right flank, which A has parried by position 4. B then renews the attack by bringing his point over A's blade and lunging again to the knee. A follows B's blade with his own, making his point describe a complete circle anti-clockwise and returning again to position 4. A has now completed the circular parry.

Fig 17

Circular Parry from position 5

Exactly as from position 4, only on the left side from position 5. This time A's point follows B's in a clockwise direction. Circular parries are best employed not on their own but as part of a sequence.

Taking Control of the Opponent's Blade

This is the action of binding the opponent's blade, and the move can be carried out from each parry position. The effect is to add greater flamboyancy and variety to the blade patterns, but the logic is an attempt to disarm. The method is to parry the attack, then straighten the blade to form a line with the arm, and swing the opponent's blade to the opposite side. As with circular parries, the bind is most effectively

employed not on its own, but as part of a sequence. The safest positions for the beginner to undertake these manoeuvres from are the two shoulder parries, and next the two head parries. Unless an actor is experienced, binding from the two flank parries should be avoided, as there is a danger of carrying the opposing point in front of the face. Besides this, enveloping or binding from the flank positions is often too large, giving an amateurish appearance.

It is worth noting in all movements of this kind that the art is to

Fig 18a

Fig 18b

Fig 19a

Fig 19b

Fig 20

catch the half of the opponent's blade nearest the point with the half of one's own blade nearest the guard, and a necessary 'cheat' is for the attacker to keep his arm straight during the course of the movement, for if it is bent there is the possibility of losing blade-contact. Examples of envelopments can be seen in Figures 18a and b, and 19a and b.

Sidestep Evasions *(Figs 20, 21, 22 & 23)*

Avoidances or evasions were in common practice in early rapier play, and can be theatrically effective as part of a sequence. At the time when they were in use the idea was to avoid the oncoming attack, while at the same time stretching out the sword arm in the direction of the adversary to run him through. For our purposes the latter is not at all a good idea, for reasons which will be apparent, and in avoiding an attack the weapon is best taken away from the 'opposition'!

Avoidances are executed by one definite movement of the foot, as shown in the illustrations, rather than by a shuffle or jump which will place one off balance for any following movement. By using these sidesteps it is possible to come straight back to the basic position again by merely reversing the action in one clean movement when the attack has been avoided.

Cuts

Fundamentally, cuts may be made to five definite parts of the opponent's body — to the head, to the right and left shoulders, and to the right and left flanks. As explained previously, cutting attacks should be made lightly, and strength should never be used. Apart from the safety factor, it is far harder to parry and return the opponent's reply if weight has been put into the original attack. To say that attacks must be made lightly does not of course mean that they need to *appear* half-hearted. It looks unreal to see the attacker's arm not fully extended, and when it is bent there is also the danger of contact not being made, due to the attack being short.

In making any cut it is important that equal time value should be given to the preparation (the backward arm movement prior to the attack). This sets up a rhythm which is an aid to safety.

An obvious point, but one which needs to be made, is that the cut should always be made with the edge of the blade and never with the flat.

Cut to Head *(Fig 24)*

The preparation for the head cut is made by lowering the sword and swinging the arm either across the chest or behind the back in a circular motion, finally bringing the blade down vertically to meet the parry. At the end of the action the wrist will be flexed, thereby 'pulling' the stroke. The whole action should be smoothly executed.

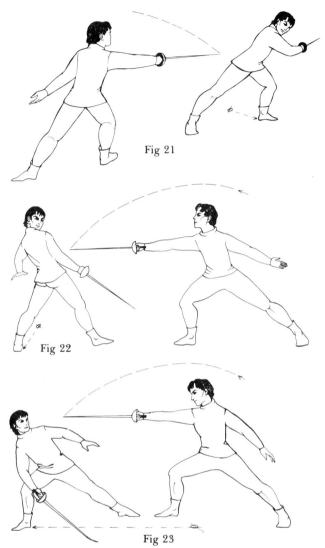

Fig 21

Fig 22

Fig 23

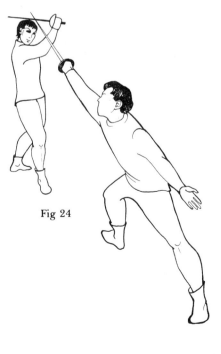

Fig 24

Cuts to Shoulder *(Figs 25 & 26)*

The principle here is the same as for the cut to the head, in that there is a smooth preparation of the sword arm (this time bending the arm from the elbow at shoulder-height), while the wrist relaxes back and flexes just before the contact. Try to make the stroke travel parallel to the ground and never diagonally, for one which starts high and ends up low, or vice versa, is potentially unsafe. When aiming at the right shoulder of the 'opponent' the palm will be turned down, and in cutting to the left shoulder the palm will be turned up.

Cuts to Flank *(Figs 27 & 28)*

Make the cut in the same way, by bending the arm back in preparation, this time at flank-height and flexing the wrist for the hit. Again, as with shoulder cuts, if you are attacking to the right the palm will be turned down, and if to the left, up. The action as with the shoulder cuts should be made to travel horizontally, but starting at the lower height.

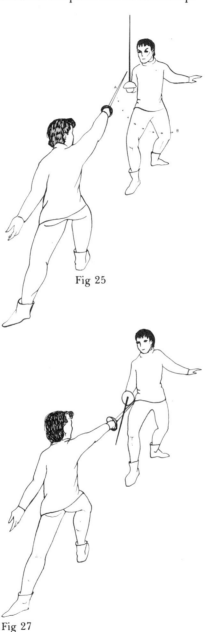

Fig 25

Fig 27

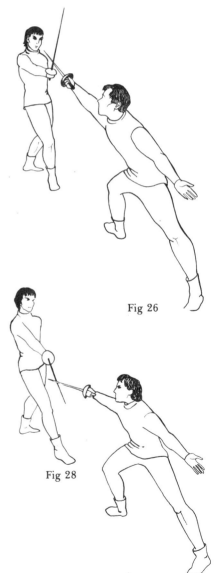

Fig 26

Fig 28

The Thrust

Although the manner of the preparation can vary to disguise an often boring move, the thrust with the point is made by a smooth extension of the arm, usually followed by the lunge. For the beginner it should be made only in low line, to be met by the two flank parries, aiming a little above knee-height. Care should be taken that this comes neither higher nor lower. The point must travel absolutely in a straight line from a to b, for nothing is worse for the receiver than a thrust which is waggling about as it moves to the target. To repeat, unless you are experienced never use a thrust above waist-height.

With the arrival of the small-sword in the late seventeenth century, point work predominated, but to limit moves in a play of this period to thrusts in the low line would be unrealistic. For safety, though, the techniques of coping should be learnt under the guidance of a professional master.

Ducking a Cut to Right or Left Shoulder *(Fig 29)*

The cut to either shoulder will be executed in the manner previously described, but it will obviously carry on, as it meets no parry. The important thing is to keep the cut travelling shoulder-height the whole way through the action, running parallel to the floor. If the cut is coming at any sort of angle it is harder to avoid with confidence of safety. When making a cut that is to be ducked prepare the stroke by bending the elbow at shoulder-height and taking the blade behind the shoulder. This will give the opponent a beat — a moment — in which to prepare for his evasion, and the move itself will have more impetus. There are various means of avoiding, but the simplest is to place the left hand on the floor, while shooting the left

leg straight back and tucking the head right down. The head should always be turned away from the direction of the cut, thereby ensuring complete safety. The only exception is, of course, when one has extremes in height, and a tall man has to duck, while a short man makes the cut. If this is the unfortunate situation, it might well be best to avoid the movement altogether!

Fig 29

Footwork

Excluding turning movements, side-steps and avoidances, characters fighting with swords are going to lunge out and back from a set, safe distance and move forward and backward. The essential requirement is to maintain a safe distance at all times, and this can be achieved provided that footwork is planned to marry with the sword strokes. When a single attack is launched the defender need not move, but if the attacker is to advance the defender in order to keep distance must take a corresponding number of steps back. To summarize, while one is actually trading blows (as against running or moving about) every step and move should be planned, and never allowed to vary.

Body Movements with Heavy Weapons

In using very heavy weapons (e.g., double-handed swords) it is more effective when there is greater move-

31

ment of the body. For instance, if in preparation for a cut to the head one only makes the swing from the elbow the true effect of the weight of the sword is lost (Fig 30). The body must be behind the movement (Fig 31), for whether the weapons are in fact heavy or not, if they are big the movements will only look real if the effect of weight is behind them. With large and heavy weapons it will be found necessary to take a larger preparation with every attack (i.e., a swing into the attack). In other words, the supposed weight of the weapons should be 'acted through' with the body.

Four Parries for use with Rapier and Dagger

These are used to parry a cut to the head, a thrust to the stomach, a cut to the waist on the right, and a cut to the waist on the left. They should all be made with the arms straight and pushed forward and away from the body, maintaining as wide an angle as possible between the blades of the rapier and dagger in which to catch the opponent's blade. It is possible to move from one parry to any of the others without repositioning the blades and hands. For parrying the cut to the head (Fig 32), the palms will be three-quarters on to the opponent. For parrying a thrust to the stomach, the knuckles will be facing the opponent (Fig 33). In parrying a cut to the waist on the right, the palms will be away from the opponent (Fig 34) and towards him on the left side (Fig 35).

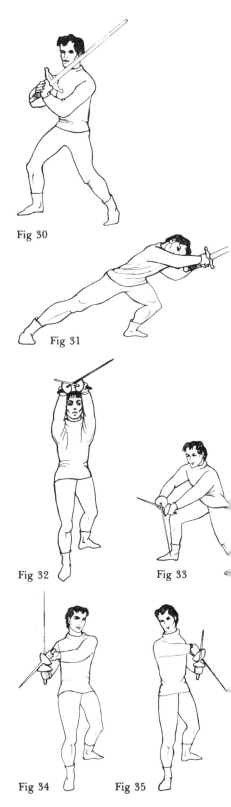

Fig 30

Fig 31

Fig 32

Fig 33

Fig 34

Fig 35

The following pages show a selection of photographs
of fight scenes from stage and film productions.

EARLY STAGE PRODUCTIONS

'The Country Manager
Rehearses a Combat'.
Etching by Phiz of the
Crummles Family for
Nicholas Nickleby by
Charles Dickens.

An operatic feel to the
famous duel, seemingly
displaying a singular lack of
urgency.

The duel scene from *Hamlet*
during Forbes Robertson's
Farewell Season at the
Theatre Royal, Drury Lane,
1913.

As in so many early photos
of fight scenes, the look here
is posed and unanimated.
The difficulty must have
been keeping still in awkward
positions while waiting for
the photographer. Legs
must certainly have ached
after a photographic session!

Martin Harvey as Don Juan
defends himself from a
double attack in *Don Juan's
Last Wager*, Prince of
Wales Theatre, 1900.

A splendid lesson to reluctant actor/fighters. Looking at this picture, it is easy to appreciate why such plays as *The Fencing Master's Daughter* were written for Victorian theatre!

Esmé Beringer, who died only a few years ago in her nineties; the play — *At the Point of the Sword*, 1901.

Combatants of supposed
equality: the posed look
again. This is the type of
cliché lock position which
used normally to be
accompanied by a line of
dialogue of the 'You've come
to Sherwood once too often'
variety!

Matheson Lang as Romeo
fights with Halliwell Hobbs,
Tybalt, in *Romeo and
Juliet*, Lyceum Theatre,
1908.

Rigid positions — oh, the aching legs! If required to move, I wonder if this couple would be able to at all — although, judging by their finery, they were probably quite flamboyant movers.

Eric Mayne, Frederick Ross and Matheson Lang in *The Prisoner of the Bastille*, Lyceum Theatre, 1909.

'These foils have all a length?' Trouser length may be more the problem!

Frank Vosper, Dorothy Massingham, Colin Keith-Johnson, Robert Holmes and Guy Vivian in *Hamlet* in modern dress, Kingsway Theatre, 1925.

MODERN STAGE PRODUCTIONS

Reach and stretch out! The look of real intention in the attack. A good distance between the two, and Mercutio bends down low. *Photo Rolf Linder.*

Hans Henrik Voetmann and Per Moller Mielsen as Mercutio and Tybalt in the Odense Theatre production of *Romeo and Juliet,* Denmark, 1978.

As in the last photograph,
costumes and weaponry (the
light cup-hilt rapier) by
their lightness, facilitate
movement.

Peter O'Toole (Hamlet) and
Derek Jacobi (Laertes) in
Laurence Olivier's National
Theatre production of
*Hamlet. Photo Angus
McBean.*

Half-hearted combatants
and, understandably, no
proper stance from either.
Viola's legs together and
bottom back posture tell the
story of her reluctance.
Likewise with Aguecheek —
a position which could
hardly be called aggressive!

David Warner as Aguecheek
(left) and Diana Rigg as
Viola in *Twelfth Night*,
Royal Shakespeare
Company's production at
Stratford-on-Avon, 1966.
Photo Gordon Goode.

Man versus machine. Back
to back, Faust and
Mephistopheles revolve,
swords whirling, like an
impregnable robot.

Faust Part One at the
Residenz Theater, Munich.
Director Michael Degen.
*Photo Jean-Marie
Bottequin.*

The reality and muddy
effect of Shakespearean
battle. No stylized
formations, as in the next
two photographs.

Coriolanus, Royal
Shakespeare Company,
Stratford-on-Avon. Central
figure, Ian Hogg in the title
role.

The formalized crowd reactions here of the ballet version contrast sharply in the use of crowds, both with the previous picture of *Coriolanus* and the realistic treatment in Zeffirelli's *Romeo and Juliet* on page 50.

Left to right: Benvolio (Anthony Dowell), Romeo (Rudolf Nureyev), Mercutio (David Blair) and Tybalt (Desmond Doyle) in the Royal Ballet's production of Kenneth MacMillan's *Romeo and Juliet. Photo Houston Rogers.*

Vibrant stylization! The
almost dance-like
choreography of the
massacre by Claude
Chagrin.

The National Theatre's
production of *The Royal
Hunt of the Sun. Photo
Angus McBean.*

Revolutionary realism.
Young protagonists in heavy
and realistic jerkins (no
lightweight shirts)
performed with full acted
aggression.

Franco Zeffirelli's legendary
production of *Romeo and
Juliet* at the Old Vic
Theatre, London. *Left to
right:* Alec McCowan
(Mercutio), John Stride
(Romeo) and Tom
Kempinski (Tybalt).

The heavy brigade! Macbeth
and Macduff in
performance show the effect
of the actual weight of
armour and weaponry. Only
the truly dedicated could
cope with all this!

Albert Finney as Macbeth
(left) and Daniel Massey as
MacDuff in Peter Hall's
production at the National
Theatre, 1978. *Photo
Nobby Clark.*

FILM COMBATS

The start of the combat —
fully equipped with sword
and axe, shield and sword,
Macbeth and Macduff
battle in Polanski's film.

Terence Bayler as Macduff
(left) and Jon Finch as
Macbeth.

Near to the end. Now exhausted — axe, shield and sword are gone (possibly teeth too!). Weapons striking against fully armoured bodies, instead of blade simply meeting blade, give a thudding reality to the combat, in keeping with the reality of the film.

Terence Bayler as Macduff (left) and Jon Finch as Macbeth.

Film rehearsal. Special
effects man in the air!

The Prince and the Pauper.
1977 version.

The tongue-in-cheek reality
of *The Three Musketeers.*
Oliver Reed recovers from a
kick in the crotch, while
Michael York moves in to
the rescue! Heavy weapons
true to the period together
with truthful costuming
help to get away from the
swashbuckling look of
before.

The Three Musketeers,
director Richard Lester.

Bloody and savage. No early
Hollywood stuff here! Long,
heavy military sabres were
used for Ridley Scott's prize-
winning film at Cannes.

The Duellists. Director
Ridley Scott. Harvey Keitel
as Feraud (left) and Keith
Carradine as D'Hubert.
Photo Paramount Pictures.

Double trouble! The conclusion of a tavern fight in the German film *Tod Oder Freiheit* based on Schiller's play *The Robbers.*

Regina Zeigler production, 1977.

Plenty of cloaks, which were
used as a protection to the
left arm, in this
Cassio/Montano brawl.
Lightweight cross-hilt swords
of the period were used.

Derek Jacobi (Cassio) and
Edward Hardwicke
(Montano) in the brawl
scene from the British Home
Entertainments film based
on John Dexter's National
Theatre production of
Othello.

Unarmed combat: a kick to the face. The recipient holds his hands at chest level, one over the other, with thumbs in. The attacker kicks (pointing his toes) the hands with the upper part of his foot. Note that the attacker is placed on a box to give height, while his left hand has a firm grip, which is necessary for stability. The recipient is falling backwards, in order to perform with the greatest speed and effect, on to a mattress (unseen by the camera), which protects his head.

Jack Barry in the BBC television production of *Night Out,* an episode in the *Z Cars* series. *Photo Odhams Press.*

More unarmed combat in a rehearsal of *Romeo and Juliet* for the Residenz Theater, Munich.

A sequence of blade strokes performed by two combatants — the patterns recorded by the addition of tiny bulbs to the tips of the blades. Variety in the planning of strokes leads to pictorially vibrant pictures and shapes as displayed here. *Photo Chris J. Arthur.*

8. Battle Scenes, Mass Fights, Brawls and the Like

Although it is of course impossible to re-create an entire battle on stage, it is quite feasible to reproduce the feeling and mood of a mass conflict. We are dealing here with the creation of an illusion. A number of soldiers apparently engaged in mortal combat, appearing from the wings and battling their way across the stage, only to reappear moments later to make a similar foray in the opposite direction, just won't do any more. Yet one still sees it — an ill-thought-out relic, perhaps, of Victorian theatre. How can it suggest a battle of enormous magnitude raging over a considerable distance? So what are convincing alternatives?

In the first place, to generalize about scenes of mass combat is as flippant as to do so when dealing with duels between individual characters. In a battle scene little may be known about the characters of individual fighters, as sometimes is the case, but such a scene is written to make a point, or various points, that have to be observed and shown. Every brawl, battle scene or whatever is unique, and has its own story which has to be told. The opening brawl in *Romeo and Juliet* is an excellent example, as it possesses a very clear structure. Initially we have the scrap between the servants of the Capulet and Montague households — the lower orders emulating their masters and following the dictates of the ancient vendetta. This leads into Tybalt's set-to with Benvolio, and finally we see the effect of the feud upon the citizens of Verona, who themselves become involved in the fray. Of course, it is true that until the moment when everyone is caught up in the action we are in fact concerned with separate combats with named characters, but when the scene accelerates into a general brawl we know already a great deal about the different factions. This particular brawl has a very clear story-line and character of its own.

However, allowing that each mass fight has its own particular qualities and character, large numbers brawling or fighting on stage will demand certain techniques which apply to most situations. For example, safety requires one golden rule. No one should be allocated to any other's space while actively engaged, for it only needs one actor wielding a weapon to stray into another and cause an accident. Then again, at any moment when the combatants are involved in sword-play of any kind, they should be given plenty of space in which to work freely and without hindrance, so as to be able to perform with the necessary acted aggression, without the fear of perhaps connecting with an unfortunate third party.

Not all brawls need large numbers of participants to create the illusion of size, and when the company is not large it is quite possible by careful manipulation and use of those available to create the effect and feeling of commotion. In fact, by giving less numbers greater use of the playing area, the objective can sometimes be more successfully achieved. Of course, with greater attention devoted to individuals and smaller groups of combatants, the selection of what they actually do will need to be considered with great care. There is in fact a lot to be said for conserving the numbers on-stage fighting in a brawl or battle, for the more who are involved, the greater the likelihood of strokes being hampered and movements restricted. When the effect needs to be wild, and this is minimized through fear of a possible accident, the whole sweep of the action will be lost, owing to moves being executed in a tentative fashion. In order for acted fury to be given full vent, it is essential to have freedom of movement and plenty of performing space. Strokes can then be made with full intention, and without fear. This is vital, for nothing looks worse than half-hearted movements. Strokes can be planned to go in any direction, provided always that a clear space to accommodate the move is allowed at the moment when it is made. There are naturally those occasions when a play will demand that many people should be involved, and the method here is to separate in some way, and at the vital moment, those using weapons from those without. Armed fighters should be given more space in which to perform, and those fighting without arms confined to a smaller proportion of the playing area. I am talking here in basic terms, for there are naturally times when the two will merge. It is also possible with large numbers to limit the amount of actual fighting to the minimum, while making greater use of more general movement, which can be treated either individually or en masse.

The basic task which has to be done in preparing any ensemble fight scene is to time everything so that all the pieces of the jigsaw fit, while planned incidents and moments of importance are given prominence. Here again, only incidents which are wholly convincing to the action and relevant to the plot can be selected. What are the needs of the scene, and how can those needs best be met? Finding the answers is the fascination and challenge of creating such a scene, and the result must be provided according to the require-

ments of the play, imaginatively realized.

In most brawl scenes positions will often change, and the audience's attention will be directed to various incidents of importance on different parts of the stage. As with straightforward duels, it is necessary with mass altercations to find changes of focus and to introduce unexpected events, thus avoiding monotony. These will naturally always be in keeping with the mood of the scene and requirements of the play.

After the initial blocking of moves, there will inevitably be gaps in the action, where one group may have completed a sequence before another group with whome they are required in some fashion to link up. This may not always matter, provided that in those gaps acting intention is continued, for it is only when an actor ceases acting, waiting for his next routine, that a gap will be apparent to an audience. On the other hand, if it adds to the effect required those gaps can be filled by action, and any actor left with 'egg on his face' can be given something to do. At the risk of repeating myself, one cannot make rules regarding creativity, but only regarding technique and safety. Each individual scrap or fight will be synchronized with everything else happening on stage, and individual combats planned and rehearsed in the usual painstaking manner. However, it is only when the overall combat has been put together that it will be possible to find out which strokes and moves need to be changed according to safety and effect. The overall plan will naturally be worked out in advance, but the detailed work will develop in the course of rehearsal.

Only when the various individual routines have been thoroughly rehearsed, and when the actors are fully conversant with their moves and positions, will it be possible for the total action to be put together and speeded up with safety. At the end of the rehearsal period, and when the play is in performance, it will be the actors' responsibility to ensure safety, by keeping faithfully to what has been rehearsed.

It is of course essential that sufficient preparation time is given to any fight. Without it precision, and safety, cannot be guaranteed, and spontaneity and danger will be more a reality than an appearance. Finally, as with all combats, it is vital to rehearse before every performance, and no truly professional actor would dream of going on stage without having done so. Just as a dancer will limber up before a show, so must an actor loosen up and revise his routine. The timing and rhythms have to be constantly rediscovered with his 'adversary'. No performance of a fight can be gone into cold when the scene arrives, because the body, even though well trained, just will not be capable of following at speed what the mind is telling it to do. The brain, as well as the muscles, needs warming up towards performance pitch. It takes, as the song says, 'two to tango', so it is not sufficient for one participant only to know and practise his routine. He will not be performing on his own, and it is necessary for all parties involved to achieve a physical harmony *together*. Failure to 'warm up' can be an invitation to disaster — perhaps not involving an accident, but certainly producing the likelihood of a poor-quality and scrappy performance.

9. Non-Realistic Fights

So far, we have been concerned only with fights of a realistic nature. There are, however, other types of combat requiring very different treatment. For example, fights to music; comic fights; and symbolic fights.

Fights to Music

Here I am referring to a fight which is really a dance, when the movements of bodies and blades adhere strictly to the rhythm of the music. The Georgian State Dance Company have in their repertoire brilliant sword dances in which the dancers make exciting exchanges in perfect time to a very fast rhythm. Another example of this type of non-realistic fight was to be seen in the renowned Berliner Ensemble production of *Coriolanus,* in which armies came together to the crash of cymbals, parted slowly, and the vanquished then sank to the ground one by one to the beat of the music. The warriors faced each other silently in two lines as the stage revolved, took them halfway round, whereupon to rhythm a further onslaught took place.

As soon as a fight is set to music it is almost bound to become unrealistic, even when the actual planning of the moves may be real enough, and not enlarged from life in any way. It is practically an impossibility for the natural speed of the actors' movements not to be held up or speeded up in some way to fit in with predetermined rhythms. In a fight to music, where the rhythm of the music determines the speed at which the fight is set, it is vital to get to know the music from the very beginning in order that the correct rhythms may be assimilated and methodically rehearsed, albeit at a slower tempo for safety. If a fight to music should go wrong by a missed move or beat, it will not be easy in performance to get back to the right place again. If it is not necessary to keep to the beat of the music it will be much simpler, as a phase can be begun again or continued without upsetting the total flow of the fight. Musical accompaniment cannot be stopped and started at will; therefore a mistimed move could throw a fight into chaos if it should cause the action to fall behind the music.

This, of course, need not deter anyone from deciding upon such an approach if it is appropriate, for there is no doubt that in the case of certain combats their effect can be excitingly heightened by the use of sound accompaniment.

Comic Fights

It is very difficult to talk in general terms about comic fights, as the construction and presentation depend so much on the situation and the characters of participants. Whether a fight succeeds in being comic or not depends on the arranger and the actors, but ultimately it will be a poor contrivance if it is not based on the truth of the scene. Often the comedy is inherent to the situation, and the fight itself will be played and planned more or less realistically. Of course, there are certain moves which are in themselves inherently funny, but again only in a correct situation and context. The comedy of these particular moves can be put down to the cliché element and they are in essence fight gags, corny because they have been witnessed countless times before. Still, performed in an unexpected fashion, they can even now make an audience laugh. Invariably, as in all arrangements, much of what is finally shown to an audience will not have been entirely created in early rehearsals, for some ideas will be scrapped and new incidents will replace them. In fact, the normal creative process.

First-rate examples of comic altercations occur in *The Venetian Twins* by Goldoni. In this play Lelio the fop has been paying court to Beatrice, one of the joint heroines, and fights with Florindo, the friend of the hero Tonino, who acts in the fight on Tonino's behalf. Lelio wins this encounter by accident rather than by skill, when Florindo slips over. Tonino himself enters to find his friend fallen on the ground and at the mercy of Lelio, who is about to deliver the *coup de grâce*. He challenges and fights the now fearful Lelio, whom he disarms. Lelio's immediate relief, displayed by his line 'What confounded luck! I'm unarmed!' speaks volumes, and such a scene, with so clear-cut a situation and with such unlikely opponents, presents the arranger of the fights with a wealth of opportunity for comic invention.

Symbolic Fights

One would usually decide upon a symbolic approach in the presentation of a fight where it is in keeping with the concept of a particular production. However, it need not be out of place to use symbolic treatment within a realistic production, and in certain cases it can extend the scope of the combat, setting it completely apart from the rest of the play and giving it a greater dramatic effect. On the other hand, one might decide on a stylized approach for reasons of sheer practicality — for example, when, as I have sometimes experienced, the fight in *Macbeth* is to be performed by a woefully out-of-condition middle-aged actor, past his physical prime, who has difficulty even lifting his sword, let alone using it! The main reason, though, for employing stylization in the presentation of a fight is to escalate the drama, and to enable the presentation to lift to a more telling effect, by removing it from the precincts of our common experience. The necessity arises in certain instances, when the effect required could not possibly be presented with enough power in normal realistic terms. For a fight to be symbolic the fight impressions or feeling have be to be shown, as opposed to an actual set-to.

This can be done in any amount of ways. For example, the whole sequence can be slowed down to lend more poignancy to the action, and to show more clearly the macabre savagery of movements. Alternatively, additional moves can be invented which depict the feeling of combat, outside the actual play.

Certain kinds of stylization have one great advantage, and that is safety. For instance, in slow motion, or when working out of distance, there is absolutely no reason for accidents. Also there is the additional advantage that body movements can be seen to better effect, and more exciting and adventurous movements achieved. A very good example of the use of stylization in fights was the massacre in Peter Shaffer's original stage production of *The Royal Hunt of the Sun* at the National Theatre, choreographed by Claude Chagrin (see photo section). The treatment was in reality a dance, and it conjured up the horrific spectacle of Incas being savagely murdered by Pizarro and his band of Spanish invaders. In theatrical terms (however brilliantly contrived and executed) no amount of realism could have as effectively conveyed the dreadfulness of such a scene.

In this country it seems to be the vogue at present for battle scenes to be more symbolic in treatment, and this can be exciting, but probably best realized in major theatre companies with sufficient time to rehearse, as the demands on the physique and the rhythmical abilities of those involved are exacting. Symbolism succeeds where it feeds the imagination of the audience to an extent that realism cannot hope to do.

Sound Effects and Music Backing

Performed in virtual silence, most fights give the effect of watching a silent film without the support of the pianist. Just as he was once needed to add mood and excitement to a film, so do most fight scenes, whether on the stage, in films, or on television, need some kind of auditory aid. It may be only vocal from the actors on stage, or on the other hand it could be necessary to have a complete musical underscore. It might be alarm bells, the amplified clash of steel, or the taped sounds of a town coming to life at the on-stage skirmish. The range of possible sound effects is exciting, particularly when electronic aids are available. Even on the slenderest budget there are numerous ways to produce stunning sound effects in keeping with the situation, which must, as always, determine all.

With battle scenes the most common form of accompaniment is percussion, for the harsh sounds of cymbal and drum are in accord with the subject, and setting a fight to sounds of this kind can add greatly to the excitement. Thus music or sound backing can accentuate and heighten the mood, and stimulate the audience's imagination. Its function is to reinforce the overall concept. It is often necessary, I believe, with any kind of sound backing to create elaborate and extravagant movements, so that the sound accompaniment never becomes more important than the action. If the movement is not 'sizeable' and full-blooded there is the danger of it being in a lower key, and in fact merely supporting the sound. The action must always be the senior partner, although of course one must complement the other.

It should perhaps be said finally that sound or music support need not necessarily be confined to battle scenes, for individual duels which are not intended to be completely realistic can also be aided by music and sound effects where appropriate.

10. Historical Accuracy

It is an essential part of the arranger's task to give consideration and proper attention to the period in which a play is set. Weaponry, and to a certain degree fashion in dress, dictates the way people move and fight, and over the years these have undergone considerable change. Duelling itself differed in style not only from country to country, but from century to century. For instance, the stance or 'on guard' position was different a hundred years ago from its modern fencing counterpart. Besides being aware of differences in costume, position and moves, it is well worth taking note of clothing accessories of a particular time, for these could perhaps be brought into use in the planning and execution of a fight.

Of necessity, authenticity must always play a secondary part to what is theatrically acceptable to a modern audience. If a fast-moving fight is required in a particular play, and the correct stance and weaponry of the period tend to hamper movement, then it is best to compromise, as long as one is not being totally untruthful to the times. As truthful as possible an *impression* of a particular period, based on accurate and careful research, is the acceptable solution. For example, while weapons should look authentic, they do not have to be of the correct weight, where this might hamper or slow down the performance. I think one must assume that fighters in whatever period choose a heavy weapon because they are physically capable of wielding it to advantage: if not, there is little point in being armed with it! This being the case, if a modern actor is given an authentic heavy weapon of the right period he will look rather silly when he tries to use it, if he is untrained and endowed with a less powerful physique than the character he is portraying. A slightly-built actor saddled with a large weapon will lend a speculative quality to the play, but it may not be quite what the dramatist had in mind when he wrote the piece.

With regard to the authenticity of movements, the long rapier of the Elizabethan period was not used for parrying, since it was too heavy, and the left-hand (Maingauche) dagger or cloak was brought into play for this purpose. However, a stage fight of this period will be severely limited choreographically if this accuracy is adhered to completely. Speed of movement again depends on the situation, but it is possible in certain cases to be fairly faithful to the period, and yet maintain an excitement which is not dependent on fast exchanges. A slow-paced fight, very much true to the period — as for example in the Middle Ages, when weapons and apparel were altogether heavier and more cumbersome than in, say, the seventeenth, and eighteenth centuries — can have a macabre savagery in itself very effective.

Since little is recorded about very early methods of parry and attack, the best method of preparation is to study old paintings and prints of a period. Small details will be discovered from these pictures which should give the end-product something of the feeling and flavour of the times. For research purposes, old prints, woodcuts and armouries are without doubt a great aid, and it is wise to seek them out, because even if they cannot offer a complete guide as to how movements were made, they will be a valuable source of knowledge, giving perhaps some idea of how the weapons of those days were held, and positions of the body, thus indicating basically how they might have been used.

It should be remembered, however, when viewing pictures of a particular period, that many of these show the ornate swords and impedimenta of noblemen and princes. The weapon of the common man and soldier would have been markedly cruder — the sword being to a large extent a symbol of status. One must also take into account an artist's often heroic impression, particularly of war scenes.

Finally, a word about stage armour. Victorian theatre used real armour on stage, which could be seen in London to as late as 1930 in the children's play *Where the Rainbow Ends*. Later, papier-mâché was used for helmets, and then whole suits of armour were made of felt and papier-mâché. The lightness must have been an enormous relief to actors, but there is something to be said for the real thing. Movements in metal armour are often more effective than in a fake lightweight suit, for the opportunity of making cuts safely to the opponent's body and limbs, instead of only the blade, widens the scope and increases the variety of movements used. Nowadays fibreglass is commonly used, but this too has its drawbacks — there is a lack of sound when the material is hit, and it is prone to chipping.

11. Unarmed Combat

Unless a specific martial art such as Karate, Aikido, Kung-fu or even wrestling is called for in a play, there are a number of general movements which can be useful in a great many situations which require hand-to-hand combat or a 'punch-up', either modern or period. Generally speaking, if a move fits the requirements of a scene, can be made to appear real and at the same time be executed with complete safety, then it is usable. There is no particular criterion to adhere to, and most movements in modern usage have been derived from wrestling and boxing, clown routines and tricks. Some movements, such as kicks and throws, are equally useful in weapon fights where the requirements are such as to demand the quality that the addition of such moves will give. For example, in *Romeo and Juliet* the Romeo/Tybalt fight needs the more desperate quality that kicks, punches and throws can give, whereas the Mercutio/Tybalt encounter is a far more skilled affair.

In unarmed combat, as with weapon work, success depends upon teamwork and having complete confidence in your 'opponent' — which as always can only be achieved by dedicated rehearsal. Moves must be worked out with exactly the same attention being paid to detail, precision, correct distancing and footwork. When working without weapons it should not be thought that there is less danger. Neither should it be assumed that it will be any easier to set a brawl or general rough-house — indeed, the more unruly a brawl is to appear, the more detailed it has to be.

Leaving aside for the time being the addition of any weapons such as knives, scissors, pokers, bottles, and other such instruments which might be incorporated into a brawl, unarmed combat will be mainly made up of slaps, punches, kicks, falls and throws, and it is in this order that they are examined here.

Slaps

There are a variety of ways in which slaps can be effective. They will be directed at the face or head, and regardless of whether they actually connect or not, the sound of palm against cheek is usually needed. This sound is known professionally as the 'knap', and without it the effect of the slap is lost, and the audience knows it is a spoof. There are occasions when a slap has to be made to connect, but this should be a last resort, only really necessary in theatre in the round, when masking is not possible. In cases such as this the hand delivering the blow must be kept completely relaxed, and care should be taken to avoid the heel of the hand connecting. The blow must be ridden by the recipient, and both parties should rehearse initially just out of distance so that the rhythm of the attack times exactly with the reaction of the partner's head. The direction of the reaction must of course continue in line with the opponent's swing, and the head should be completely relaxed. Should it be required for someone actually to be hit, one should never wait until the dress rehearsal or first night before trying the move out. The recipient must get used to being slapped, albeit lightly, or there will be the danger of either anticipating or tensing up — both of which could destroy the effect, and perhaps cause hurt or even injury. It goes without saying that when a slap is made to connect great care should be taken to avoid danger areas such as the ears, nose, eyes, neck and temples, as these are all parts of the head where harm could be inflicted.

The other and preferable method is to mask the supposed moment of contact from the audience by having the recipient's back to them. If full acted intention is behind the blow, and the reaction is real, an audience will believe they have seen it happen. A slap across the face inflicted by a man is essentially a follow-through movement, while for a woman it will usually come from the elbow and stop at the cheek, but again this is a generalization and depends on character and situation.

There are a number of ways of making the knap, but fundamentally it will be either against one's own body or against that of the opponent. If one is slapping with the right hand, this be done by striking a glancing blow against one's own arm or hand en route. Alternatively, it may be made against one or other of the opponent's hands, depending upon which hand the attacker is using to strike with. If the attacker is using his right hand, then the recipient should hold up his right hand at about breast-height for the attacker to hit in the course of his swing (Fig 36). Alternatively, should the attacker use his left, then the

recipient will hold his left hand up — but whichever it is, it must of course be masked to the audience (Fig 37). Should the blow be a backhander, the recipient should hold up the opposite hand to that of the attacker. Finally, the sound may be made by another actor on stage, but the timing in this instance is very difficult to synchronize, and I would not advise this method.

The slap can be made with a diagonal swing, from low to high, left to right, or right to left. Horizontal slaps in line with the face, but out of distance, are another possibility, striking the receiver's raised hand for the sound. The simplest method of all for making the knap is the old burlesque technique. In this instance the attacker makes his swing at the same time as his partner makes the noise by slapping his own hands together. For the final slap in a series, or at the end of a fight, one method is to grab the lapel or collar of the victim, then open the palm of the same hand while still holding on to the collar, and let the slap come by striking against the open palm. Of course, whatever the method, the co-ordination of reaction together with the sound effect is essential.

Fig 36

Fig 37

Punches

Most punches won't need the knap, and those that do need sound will be facial. The most effective technique is to punch past the face with the right hand while striking one's own breast with a relaxed left hand. The correct sound in this case will not be the same as for a slap. It is much more of a 'bony' sound, and may be heard by striking the fist against the heel of the palm. It should be noted that gloved hands make a better, more realistic, noise than bare hands. The successful punch again depends upon real motivation, so that the audience sees clearly the intention from the attacker and the correct reaction from the opponent. Punches may be made from very many directions, but essentially there are two kinds, either the jab or the follow-through. The reaction must naturally be in tune with the kind of blow received; for instance, a jab on the face will only necessitate a small recoil, whereas a full punch following through may send the recipient flying off balance. With any punch to the head, as with the slap, the head of the victim must follow the line of the punch. With punches to the body, it is most important that they are always pulled. In cases where a supposedly hard punch is seen to land in full view of the audience, some form of padding should be worn. Body punches will nearly always require some sound, but this is different from the knap, and will be mostly vocal, taking care not to outrage probability. Remember that a hard punch to the body will force a sharp exhalation of breath in most cases, rather than a shout, especially if the punch lands in the solar-plexus region. For either a punch of the follow-through variety or a slap, the correct distance to be from the opponent is arm's length, or further. A simple way to check this in the case of the odd punch is to measure up the distance: if right-handed, with the left hand first, before letting fly with the right, and vice versa for the left-hander. This stock method will often be seen on films and television.

Kicks

It applies equally to kicks as to punches and slaps that the recipient must know exactly where the blow will land, and the strength of the effect lies in the preparation of the kick. If the audience sees a vicious preparation, it will most certainly believe in the attack. Even more so than with punches, the attacker must always be well balanced for co-ordination, for at the moment of kicking he will be balancing upon one leg only, and should he happen to have got too close to his opponent, or is not near enough, the effect of the kick will be lost: it is not possible when balancing on one leg to adjust distance by swaying the body back or forward, as when punching. So the kicker must know by practice his exact position, as there is no room for variation.

Kicks that do not follow through are made with the *flat* of the foot and *pulled*. They may be made to the thigh, inside or outside, or to the hands of the recipient, when the effect is of a kick to the face.

In the case where the kick might be preceded by a run, landing at the required distance from one's opponent is even harder, and the steps must be worked out with great precision in order to land on the correct foot and at the right distance. Whatever happens, getting too close should be avoided at all costs. A point worth mentioning at this stage is that in a general free-for-all it is not in fact always necessary actually to make a blow connect for the result to look credible. With a lot of movement, overturning of furniture, noise, and most of all, acting intention, a spectacle of some realism can be achieved. Again, the attacker must always 'act' force and never really put strength into a blow. The *intention* of the preparation is what matters, together with the reaction of the receiver.

Falls

Correct falling needs training and skill, as do all the moves discussed, but in general terms relaxation is vital in order to avoid injury. Observe how in their ordinary play young children fall frequently, and because they do not tense up, normally come to little harm. Some general points, however, to bear in mind with regard to safety are:

When falling into a roll, always keep the head well tucked in to the chest. Maintain a balanced position until the last possible moment, for if balance is lost early in the fall it can cause unjury. One should take care not to fall on a bony part of the body — elbows, knees and the heel of the hand being particularly susceptible to damage. There is of course no reason, provided there is adequate covering by clothes, why, if an actor is required to fall regularly night after night, he should not wear felt or rubber padding on the knees or elbows to prevent them being hurt. For that matter, padding may be worn anywhere that will not show; but there is nothing worse than tell-tale bulges under a close-fitting costume!

Throws

There are a number of different techniques for throws, from a variety of positions. Some will land a person flat on the floor, while others will send him into a roll. In the latter case, the commonest procedure is to incorporate the dive roll which is executed on one arm. All the moves described, with and without weapons, could be dangerous if not learnt

properly under expert guidance, and in unarmed combat it must be stressed that throws are possibly the most dangerous for the unskilled to undertake, and should not be attempted without trained help. There are hip throws, neck throws, arm throws, the famous Irish whip and body throws of all kinds, taken from different sources, but they need in all cases careful and correct tuition and are beyond the scope of any manual alone.

Strangling

Thank goodness, not too many plays call for a strangling to take place; but a few notes may be helpful. Firstly, a premeditated killer may employ some article to assist in his design, such as a stocking, scarf or length of rope, and he is more likely to commit the crime from behind his victim. A spur-of-the-moment killer may attempt to strangle from the front. If a ligature is used the victim's death will be quick due to stoppage of the blood-flow, rather than a fight for breath. A person who is attacked in this way, whether strangled with bare hands or with a scarf, will react more or less the same way, and there are three stages in his reaction.
1. Surprise (naturally enough!).
2. Instinctive response to defend against the attack.
3. An involuntary fight for life.

If rope, cloth or the like is used, the actor should hold on to the knot himself, leaving the ligature comfortably relaxed around the neck of the 'victim'. Any kind of pressure on the neck should obviously never be used, but rather the effect of effort can be concentrated into pressing the hands together. When the action is performed with hands alone, and the assault is from the front, the attacker should put the pressure into the palm of the hands, keeping the thumbs relaxed, and press downward on the collar bone of the 'victim', and never inwards on to the neck. But whatever the case, real strength is not necessary — it must be acted.

Going on now to a brief word about the use of extra props such as bottles or scissors, it is always advisable where possible to use fakes rather than the real thing, even though use of the genuine article will undoubtedly foster a greater respect and regard for the possible danger of these instruments. If a substitute is used, the real article should if possible be established at some prior point in the play, in order that the audience will not question reality. If there is no alternative to the use of a real instrument, then a precaution which should be taken is the Sellotaping of the sharp edges of the article, be it the blades of scissors, a knife or a broken bottle. Personal fear when fighting with an instrument of the above-mentioned types (or for that matter, of any other) is likely to result in loss of co-ordination and tentatively executed moves,

therefore endangering the participants.

In conclusion, one or two very important points of a general nature.

First of all, *never* deviate in any way from what has been set in rehearsal.

Secondly, never strive for quantity, but rather for quality. A short, well-planned and well-executed brawl or fight is in every way preferable to a long, meaningless free-for-all.

Thirdly, when one has actually to be struck with an instrument, it is essential to pad the place to be hit, and it is naturally of vital importance to rehearse thoroughly, so that the blow is in the same place every time.

Finally, a tip for the inexperienced, starting work on their first unarmed fight, is to start something going in slow motion. From this, openings will be seen, and the correct reactions become apparent — so something can then be set as a basis upon which to work.

12. Fight Notation

As yet, there is no universal system of notating a fight scene. This is a pity, for a generally accepted form would be invaluable to stage managers in particular, as well as actors and arrangers. Most fight directors have their own method of writing moves down according to the way in which they work, but none of these covers every possible movement. In fact, it will be seen from the examples which follow that the main concern is with blade moves, but this is very limiting for in a great many situations a lot more is going on than simple sword strokes. How, for instance, does one write down 'woman hides under the table' except in long hand, or 'fighter half-turns whilst ducking, placing the left hand on the floor and extending the right to aim at the knee'? Only the Benesh system of Movement Notation would appear to cover all possibilities, and to learn it, involves a three-month course.

For interest's sake, I list four different systems — John Barton's, Arthur Wise's, my own and an example of the Benesh Movement Notation as used by Bronwen Curry of the London Festival Ballet.

1. John Barton (Associate Director, Royal Shakespeare Company

This system as devised and used by John Barton has the merit of being extremely clear and easy to use. The diagram shown represents the body, and two diagrams are required for each phase of action, one for each of the combatant's moves. Every move is numbered according to the order in which it occurs, and is positioned on the diagram wherever the attack or parry is made on the body. The plus sign is used to indicate an attack and the minus a parry. A move of the foot is shown by the letter 'F' in brackets, with an arrow to point the direction. John Barton claims that in most cases, provided an actor

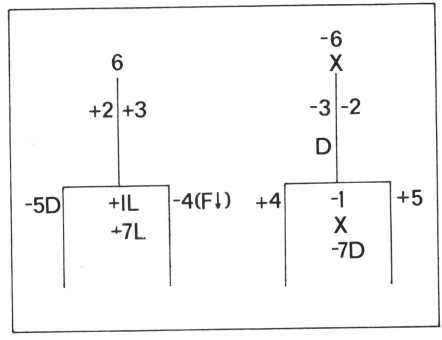

remembers the main moves through having them thus recorded, the manner in which the movement is made, and subsidiary moves will also be recalled easily.

The example below reads as follows:

Fighter A Lunges forward with a thrust.
Fighter B Parries down with a cross sword and dagger parry.
Fighter A Attacks to left shoulder.
Fighter B Parries.
Fighter A Attacks to right shoulder.
Fighter B Parries and replies with an attack to left flank.
Fighter A Parries taking the foot back.
Fighter B Attacks to right flank.
Fighter A Parries with the dagger and attacks to the head.
Fighter B Parries with crossed sword and dagger.
Fighter A Thrusts to waist.
Fighter B Parries with the dagger.

2. Arthur Wise

The basic system of Arthur Wise's notation is to separate the specific blade moves of the fighters from the more general movements over the stage area. The body is divided into various parts with each part being given a letter (A,B,C, etc.). A thrust is indicated by encircling the area aimed at, i.e. Ⓑ and a cut by a semicircle over the letter, i.e. Ⓓ. The stage area is divided also into various areas to which the fighters move, so → ☐2 indicates a general move to area 2. Solid and open rectangles are used for movements of the feet. An example of the system looks like this:

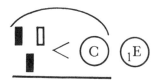

which reads:

A counter attack. The defender

moves his right foot to the left, whilst attacking to area C with a thrust, and then follows this with a dagger thrust to the right side of the abdomen.

A more extensive example of the notation looks like this:

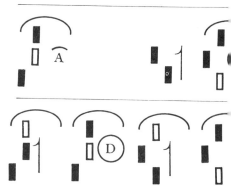

3. The Benesh Movement Notation

The extract above taken from my own sequence from the London Festival Ballet's production of *Don Quixote* was notated by Bronwen Curry F.I.Chor., and gives a discription of the body movements, stage locations, relationships of participants, identification of attacking and defending movements and exact point of blade contact.

Benesh Movement Notation was first adopted by the dance world in 1955. Today it is used by companies throughout the world for the preservation and staging of repertoires. Other applications such as Medical Research, Social Anthropology, Work Study, Ergonomics, Gymnastics and Stage Management have received less attention.

The Institute of Choreology, founded in 1963 to co-ordinate developments in all movement fields and to house a movement library, offers two full-time specialist courses and a correspondence course which introduces the principles and components of BMN as a basis for specialized study.

4. My own method

The following symbols I devised some twelve years ago and I have to admit that I now find the method not comprehensive enough for the various permutations of moves which I employ. However, for most purposes they suffice and are easily learnt. Wherever possible, an attempt has been made to make the symbol suggest the movement it represents.

Thrust	•	Parry	
Head	T	Circle	
Feints	∧	Lunge	
Envelops	�	Pushes	
Sword only	⊗	Pulls	
Jumps	⌒	Kick	
Lock	⌐	Kills/wounds	✳

Cut

R. Shoulder	Y	Ducks	
L. Shoulder	Y	Throw	
R. flank	⋀	Sidestep L.	
L. flank	⋀	Sidestep R.	

Parry and reply
Swings
Short pause
Long pause
Body to body
Moving forward

Moving back
One step forward
One step back
Deceive circular parry
Dagger only
(or any weapon in left hand)
Sword and dagger
With two hands
Punches/slaps to left cheek
Punches/slaps to right cheek
Punches to stomach
Stairs (or any higher level)
Positions reversed
Circular parry
Beat aside
Pins or pinning

Note. The parry number may be put in the symbol, i.e. 4 or 2. Parry 5 and reply would be 5, although it is, of course, clear from the attack which parry will in most cases be used. Similarly, many steps forward or back as required may be written, i.e. four steps forward would be ⋀.

A short phase using symbols

A Cuts to right shoulder
B Parries and envelops and replies with a thrust to right knee.
A Parries
B Thrusts again to right knee.

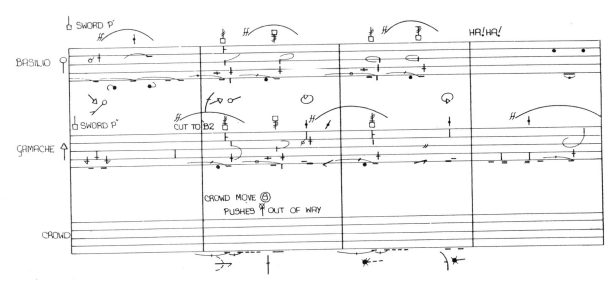

A Circular parries, beating aside and replies with a cut to the head.
B Parries and cuts to left shoulder.
A Parries and kills.

A /Ƴ, B∠↵⋏, A∠, B⋏, A0Z/T, B∠Ʋ, A∠✳

It will be seen that although covering weapon play fairly adequately for most purposes, all the systems outlined above, except the Benesh Notation, are not designed to include unarmed combat. It is mainly blade moves that are recordable; what the body is doing whilst making these moves is left out, so there is a gap to be filled. What is needed is a very simple system, easily taught to drama students, stage managers and actors, that will cover any permutation of blade and weapon strokes, together with any possible body movement, whether it be a pirouette whilst making a sword swipe, hitting some poor unfortunate over the head with a tray, or putting an arm lock on an opponent before a throw. I hope it won't be too long before such a system is devised.

13. Acting Intention and Acted Aggression

The word 'intention' is frequently used by professionals to mean the acting-through during the combat of the requisite pitch of emotion and fight aggression. Often one sees fights in plays where the level of anger and aggression displayed prior to the actual set-to is not maintained during the combat. When this happens the emotional level is dropped, and consequently the effect of reality. The involvement of the audience is suspended and the illusion is lost. I remember one 'furious Tybalt' coming back again to encounter Romeo, and the savage exchange of words shifting shamelessly at the first contact to a pat-a-cake altercation — more reminiscent of the children's game than Tybalt's threat of 'bitterest gall'. One of the most commonplace reasons why this happens is that actors have been given over-complicated movements which are beyond their basic ability. No matter how cleverly a fight is arranged, nothing is as important as its *acting*. In the performance of a combat two contradictory things are happening. On the one hand, *characters* are seen to be performing on a highly charged emotional level. On the other, the *actors* have to be working mentally on a conscious level of coolness, with complete body relaxation and control, so that their acting aggression can be performed with conviction, and at the same time in absolute safety. Always there is the danger that a certain type of actor wishing to 'put on a good show' may expose himself or his fellows to actual bodily harm, by over-zealously extending the acted 'intention' into real aggression. Like Hamlet when he complains of over-acting, such excess 'offends me to the soul', I too

would 'have such a fellow whipped'! Such actors should be reminded that real strength or fury will not necessarily come across to an audience. Some years ago I remember a certain actor at Stratford-upon-Avon who, clad in armour and in the thick of the *Coriolanus* battle, charged shouting at his 'opponent' from the back of the steeply raked stage. In the course of the attack he slipped and went skidding on his backside right past his astonished would-be combatant, right off the stage, ending up right off the stage, ending up sprawled across the lap of a bewildered spectator in the front row of the stalls — audience participation, I would say, taken to extremes! The story did not quite end there. Not only did the audience also witness the humiliating episode of the warrior scrambling ignobly back on to the stage, but also of the spectator upstaging everyone by rising from his seat and holding aloft (with certain pride) his battle-injured bloody index finger! Such an actor may feel well satisfied with his emotional involvement, but this can be dangerous, as we have seen; a cool head, technical skill and simulated emotion are far more likely to achieve the intended dramatic force of the scene.

Sequences of movements can be splendidly choreographed, and the combat devised with invention and skill, but when the acting of the fight is not at the necessary pitch of supposed aggression there will be no illusion of reality — in fact, a non-fight. Naturally, there will be some situations where the characters are non-belligerent, as in the Aguecheek/Viola scene in *Twelfth Night* but even in such skirmishes the moves must still be executed with the same care and intention, even allowing that they may have been selected for their apparent *lack of effect,* and the idea is to show up the ineffectualness of the characters.

On the whole, it is better to perform a shorter sequence well, and with acting intention behind the moves, than to drag out a longer routine in which performance level is under pitch, owing to actors being hesitant about their movement sequences. Complete control is the essential requirement, while an appearance is given of being out of control. A generalization, perhaps, but in most cases true.

14. Swords - A Brief History

Probably the first swords to be made were fashioned from spear-heads. The sword of the Bronze Age period was in reality a long knife, and because bronze is too soft to be used for blade-to-blade combat, it had to remain a thrusting weapon only, and could not be employed for cutting purposes. This 'long knife' continued to thrive in the Iron Age, when it was used against people who had no kind of armour to protect themselves. Later on, however, the Hellenes, who were possibly the first people to use a crude armour — namely shield, helmet and basic body protection — had sword edges sharpened. Thus the weapon became a cutting instrument as well as a stabbing one, able to hack through the armour of the foe. As a result the sword became broader, and therefore heavier to wield.

The use of iron swords spread across Europe, but for many centuries these swords were lacking in any form of hand protection, for the idea of parrying a cut or thrust with the sword blade had not yet arrived, due most likely to the sheer weight of the weapons. Protection of this sort did not come to Europe until about the tenth century, and at the beginning took the form of a simple cross hilt. Later on the shield was discarded in favour of a more elaborate guard for the hand, and as fighting developed into sword against sword this guard became more solid, particularly during the twelfth to fourteenth centuries.

The Middle Ages saw a diversity in the types of swords used. Broadly speaking, these could be divided into two groups: the Asiatic (Mongol, Tartar, Cossack), and the European. The former had no hand-guard to their sword at all, whereas the European fostered the guard, on the sensible principle, perhaps, that the enemy would fight back! So from the simple cross hilt of the Crusaders came a knuckle guard, and finally a fully guarded hilt. The cutting sword grew heavier and heavier until the arrival of the Italian Sciavona, which had a completely enclosed hilt; from this came the Scottish claymore of the sixteenth and seventeenth centuries, a variation of the normal Western European style. With the invention of gunpowder the armoured knight became obsolete, and with him went armour and shields. The tendency was towards a cut-and-thrust weapon — in other words, the long, narrow-bladed rapier, the hilt of which became even more protected.

By the Elizabethan age swords were reflecting the fashion of the period, and as the blades became better forged, so they were able to be more elaborate, and became 'the badge of gentlemen'. Men-at-arms carried cruder weapons, and during peace-time they were more or less forbidden to carry arms at all in public places because it was well known that ex-soldiers all too frequently took to such professions as foot-pad and highwayman.

The swords of gentlemen continued to grow more elegant in the seventeenth and eighteenth centuries, finally evolving into the small-sword. The hilts of these times were of enamel and precious metals such as gold and silver, and the blades were made of the finest steel, and were as much a part of a gentleman's dress as his lace handkerchief. However elaborately these rapiers were decorated, they were none the less formidable and highly practical weapons. About the time of Marlborough's campaigns the small-sword developed into the heavier sword of the Georgian officer, the lighter weapon being ineffectual for battle. With the development of the bayonet, it was necessary for the infantry officers to have a much more robust weapon, and the cavalry sabre made its appearance. A controversy arose in the nineteenth century over whether the sabre should be used for cutting or thrusting. In the end it was used for both.

During the French Revolution the armouries of the aristocrats were looted, and the citizens paraded with priceless small-swords. When it came to a set-to, however, they preferred to use the broad-bladed sabres with heavy curves, being completely untrained in the use of these other weapons. In the revolutionary army the rule was, the more important the officer (in his own estimation, at least!), the bigger the sword.

In the period after Waterloo, when British officers became very dandified, the dress or 'walking' sword became lighter and very thin-bladed, and of such length that it could be carried over the left arm — or alternatively allowed to drag on the ground! It wasn't very long after this that swords were abandoned as weapons of war, and the only serious use they have today is as bayonets used mainly as stabbing instruments — very much akin, in fact, to the first use for which they were made thousands of years ago!

Introductory note to sword illustrations
The weapons illustrated are a fair selection of those that can be easily hired or
still bought on the open market. They are historically authentic in essence, but
necessary adaptations have been made for use on stage.

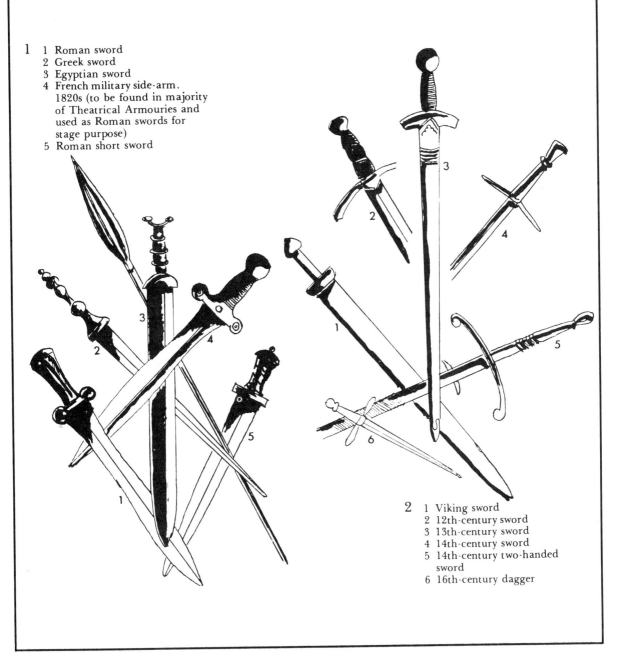

1   1 Roman sword
    2 Greek sword
    3 Egyptian sword
    4 French military side-arm,
      1820s (to be found in majority
      of Theatrical Armouries and
      used as Roman swords for
      stage purpose)
    5 Roman short sword

2   1 Viking sword
    2 12th-century sword
    3 13th-century sword
    4 14th-century sword
    5 14th-century two-handed
      sword
    6 16th-century dagger

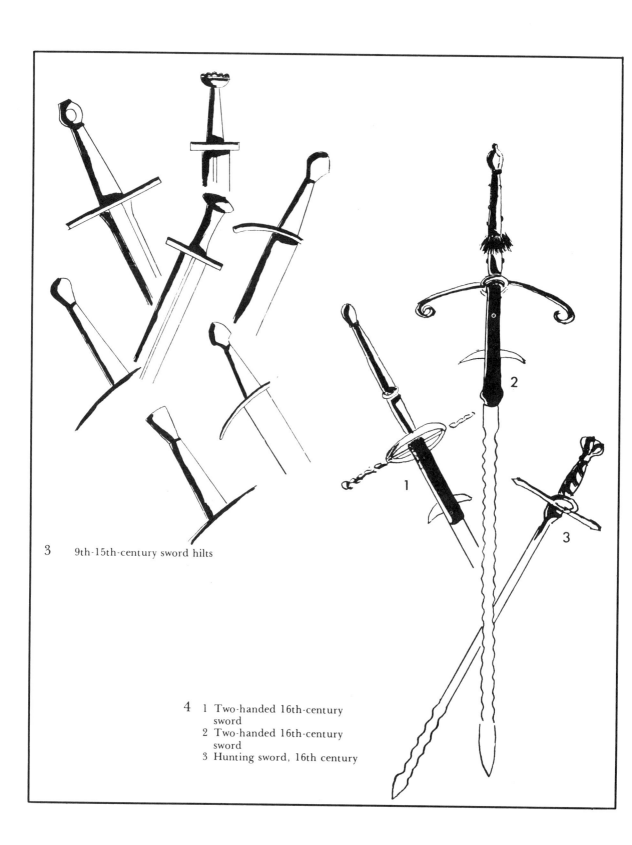

3   9th-15th-century sword hilts

4 1 Two-handed 16th-century
      sword
    2 Two-handed 16th-century
      sword
    3 Hunting sword, 16th century

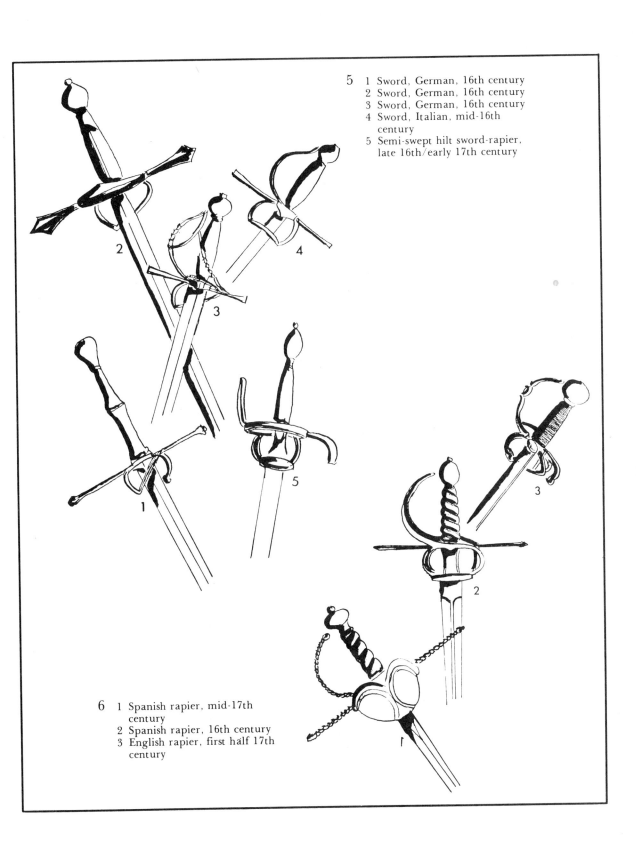

5 1 Sword, German, 16th century
   2 Sword, German, 16th century
   3 Sword, German, 16th century
   4 Sword, Italian, mid-16th
     century
   5 Semi-swept hilt sword-rapier,
     late 16th/early 17th century

6 1 Spanish rapier, mid-17th
     century
   2 Spanish rapier, 16th century
   3 English rapier, first half 17th
     century

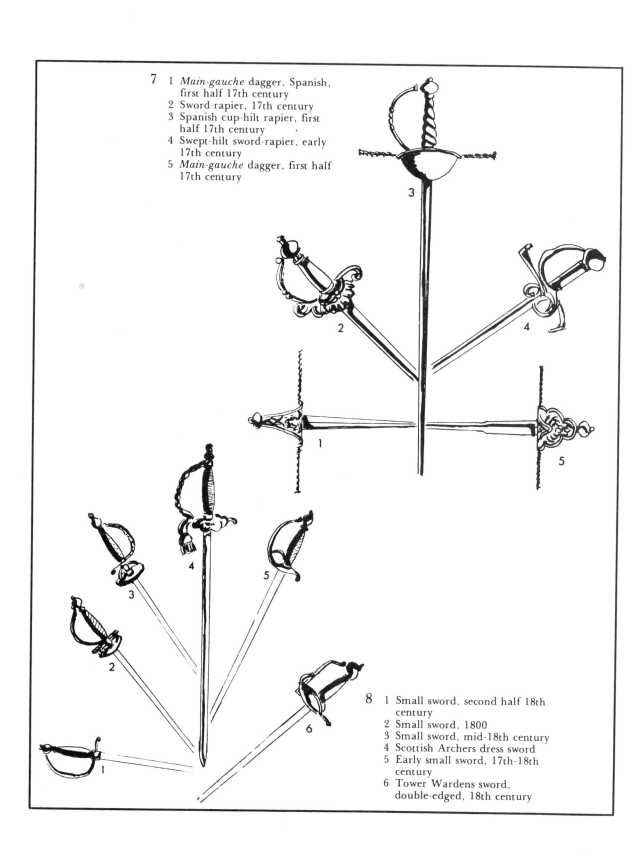

7 1 *Main-gauche* dagger, Spanish, first half 17th century
    2 Sword-rapier, 17th century
    3 Spanish cup-hilt rapier, first half 17th century
    4 Swept-hilt sword-rapier, early 17th century
    5 *Main-gauche* dagger, first half 17th century

8 1 Small sword, second half 18th century
    2 Small sword, 1800
    3 Small sword, mid-18th century
    4 Scottish Archers dress sword
    5 Early small sword, 17th-18th century
    6 Tower Wardens sword, double-edged, 18th century

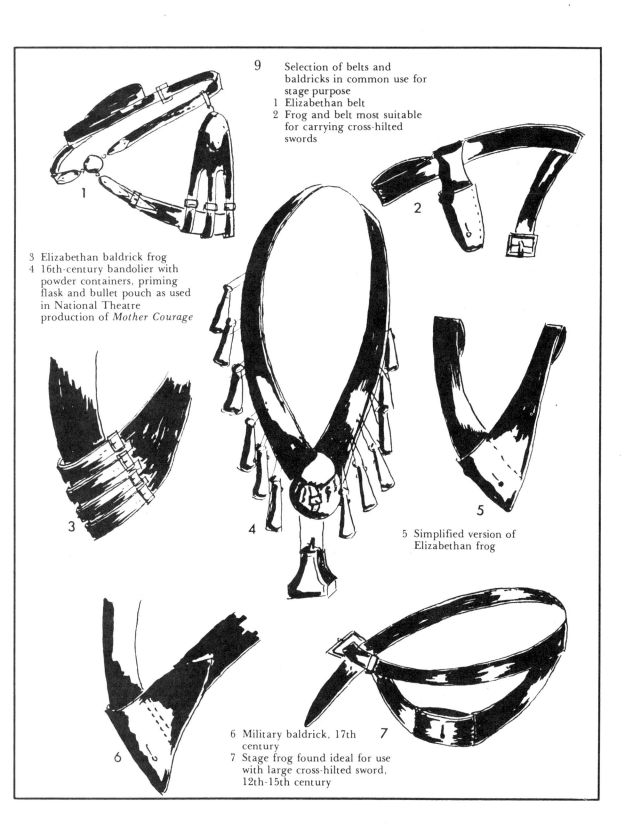

9 Selection of belts and baldricks in common use for stage purpose
1 Elizabethan belt
2 Frog and belt most suitable for carrying cross-hilted swords
3 Elizabethan baldrick frog
4 16th-century bandolier with powder containers, priming flask and bullet pouch as used in National Theatre production of *Mother Courage*
5 Simplified version of Elizabethan frog
6 Military baldrick, 17th century
7 Stage frog found ideal for use with large cross-hilted sword, 12th-15th century

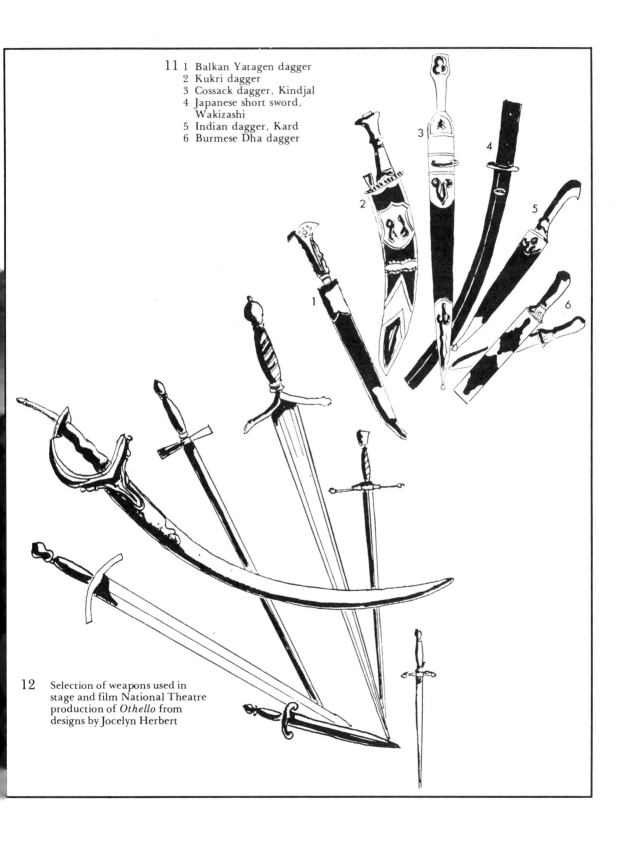

11 1 Balkan Yatagen dagger
2 Kukri dagger
3 Cossack dagger, Kindjal
4 Japanese short sword, Wakizashi
5 Indian dagger, Kard
6 Burmese Dha dagger

12 Selection of weapons used in stage and film National Theatre production of *Othello* from designs by Jocelyn Herbert

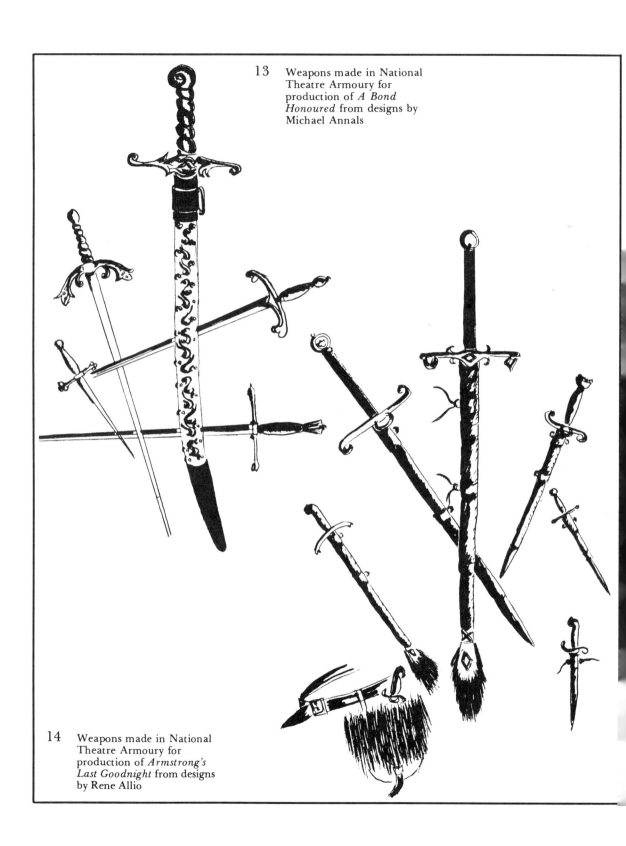

13 Weapons made in National Theatre Armoury for production of *A Bond Honoured* from designs by Michael Annals

14 Weapons made in National Theatre Armoury for production of *Armstrong's Last Goodnight* from designs by Rene Allio

15. General Information

Deaths

There are a great many moves, both armed and unarmed, which can be used convincingly on stage to depict a death, ranging from a faked blow to the head to a 'mortal' sword-thrust.

A credible result depends on acting-intention on the part of the attacker, and the reaction of the victim. With swords, the killing stroke usually needs at the right moment to be masked from the audience. It is a case of the quickness of the hand deceiving the eye. Technique plus trickery!

Use of Blood

There are, of course, those occasions when the use of blood is a necessity, and indeed the text of certain scenes, such as the murder of Julius Caesar, demands it. However, it is surprising how rare such demands are, for most deaths and woundings can be presented without blood and gore. It is not the fact that a person bleeds from a wound which is of importance for an audience, but rather how an attacker and victim react. As a shock measure only, stage blood can be effective in appropriate situations, but in a great many cases the sight of an oozing red liquid is unnecessary, and can indeed hamper belief, rather than add to it.

There are four types of theatrical blood:

1. Stage Blood, which is slow running (but very red).
2. General Purpose Blood, which is normal consistency (i.e. fairly red).
3. Blood Capsules, which contain a powder pigment and are for use in the mouth only (but, from experience, revolting to use). (See List of Suppliers.)
4. Real Blood (expensive).

Swords

If a sword, or particularly a dagger, does not have to be drawn, it should be fastened in some way to the scabbard or frog to ensure that it will not fall out.

When the historically correct sword-guard is very elaborate, or the cross bar has a pronounced downward curve, it is sometimes necessary to compromise in style; for with some weapons there is a danger when fighting of the opposing blade becoming trapped in the guard. It goes without saying that care should be taken in selecting weapons to choose those which are at the same time usable by the actors and correct for period and character.

Care of Weapons

Regular care of fighting weapons is essential. For instance, a loose hilt could prove dangerous by upsetting the balance of the sword at a vital moment. It is important also to inspect swords before each performance for notches in the blade. They often occur after use, and should be filed down to avoid gashed hands. If a blade should become so badly notched as to necessitate being ground on a grindstone, it should never be allowed to overheat, as if it does much of the temper may be lost. Rusted blades should be treated with anti-rust oil, and the oil allowed to penetrate before using abrasives. Very worn emery cloth is an ideal rust-remover and polisher. New ones tend to scratch the blade. The edges and point of a blade should never be left sharp. Edges should be blunt, and the point rounded off. I am constantly amazed that at least one well-known theatrical hire firm sends out swords for use with sharply pointed and dangerous blades. Even a blunt weapon in the wrong hands can be dangerous, and to work with sharp blades is potentially lethal.

Belts and Frogs

The right type of sword belt and frog (the attachment on the belt for carrying the scabbard and sword) play a vital part in helping the actor to carry the sword in the right position for both movement and ease of drawing. The shape of the sword hilt is the deciding factor. For example, the Elizabethan hilt (which is either a cup or a swept hilt) cannot have close contact with the hip, and will therefore always hang low and at an angle. The cross-hilt sword, on the other hand, was carried close to the body, and in the majority of cases horizontally.

Sword frogs through the ages have altered very little except in the Elizabethan period. The modern soldier's bayonet frog is indeed more or less the same shape which has carried swords through the ages. It may be noted that although invaluable as a guide, paintings depicting sword belts can be very impractical when copied for actual stage use, for some of the fussy strappings can impede movement and usage.

School Plays

When setting any kind of fight for children it is advisable to employ only a few moves which are simple and can then be rehearsed thoroughly, and so performed with safety. The safest sword strokes are simple cutting actions (particularly in low line) and avoidances. High-line thrusts should be avoided, but variety can be obtained by breaking up a phase previously used and altering the rhythm with various pauses. Creating incidents outside the sword-play and changes of

position will also help. Then the actual blade-play need only be short and simple.

Guns

1. An actor should not necessarily react to being 'shot' by a small pistol or firearm merely by dropping inert to the floor. The weapon itself may be small, but this need not entail a small reaction. A lifelike reaction will depend upon the calibre of the gun, and whereabouts on the body the bullet is supposed to have struck.
2. Even though only blanks are used, one should never on any account aim at the face, because burns can still be inflicted. A safe distance to fire from is not less than six feet (about two metres) away from the victim. An actor being shot needs to contrive that at the moment of the shooting his hands are not in front of his body, again because of the danger of burns.
3. With shotguns of the muzzle-loading variety particular care needs to be taken and the aim should be completely away from the target person.
4. If it is necessary for a gun to be fired at very close range, it is possible to hire specially prepared weapons which have the blast directed away from where one is aiming, either down or to the side. On this question of hiring, it is also possible to hire fake silencers, for a blank cannot be fired through a real silencer.

N.B. Licences for firearms *must* be obtained from the local police station. It is not necessary for the actor using the firearm to obtain a licence, but rather the stage manager or person in charge. Licences are issued entirely at the discretion of the police, and are not obtainable for any fully automatic weapons (i.e. sub-machine-guns or machine pistols).

16. Fight Clichés

To conclude, a light-hearted reminder of some of the more obvious fight clichés. In commemoration of past heroes of the blade, some of their once original ploys may be worthy of a second look. I do not advocate their re-use, or yet that they remain but glorious memories: only the actual situation can dictate what should or should not be used. Nowadays most of these tricks could be classified under the heading 'the art of coarse fighting', so the reader would be well advised to think again before using any in a serious combat situation.

1. The hilt-to-hilt lock, face to face, prior to push-away (a moment for dialogue in those splendid Flynn/Fairbanks films).

2. The flamboyant disarm.

3. The sword-thrust which just misses the opponent with the quivering blade becoming impaled in some object, making withdrawal impossible.

4. The killing thrust which goes under the arm, with the sword held grimly as if glued in position.

5. The blow, punch, kick which has no effect (all those Hollywood Westerns) — the receiver merely dusting himself down and fighting on apparently unharmed in superhuman fashion.

6. The famous slicing of the candles, in various permutations.

7. The regulation jump over the opponent's blade.

8. All slashing away up and down stairways.

9. The sword gets stuck in the scabbard when an attempt is made to draw (humorous!).

10. The foot placed on the opponent's blade, as an aid to dialogue or for a disarm.

Close observers of my work may impertinently like to add to this list. On the rack, I'd be bound to confess to a certain relish for favourite moves; of course, these are used sparingly and selectively, but if on rare occasions Romeo, Hamlet and Macbeth have all three strangely favoured my 'golf swing' with the hilt, let me put it down to their intrinsic skill and not my own lack of innovation, for after all, if a movement is right for a particular character and a particular weapon, that is what matters. As their creator himself so aptly put it, 'suit the action to the word, the word to the action'.